First On The Scene

Richard Ford

First on the Scene

Published by Insight Publishing Group
8801 S. Yale, Suite 410
Tulsa, OK 74137
918-493-1718

Copyright © 2000 by Richard Ford
Family Worship Center
910 Brand Lane
Stafford, TX 77477

Unless otherwise indicated, all Scripture quotations are
from the King James Version of the Bible.

Used by permission
Cover design by Paragon Communications

ISBN 1-930027-17-6

Library of Congress catalog card number: (number)

1.   Christian Living

Printed in the United States of America

These drawings are by Reese Ford, the ten-year old grandson of Pastor Ford. Each drawing represents how Reese sees his grandfather as the stories within this book were told to him. According to Reese his grandfather is a . . .Ghost-Buster.

It's about demons.

Paw-paw overpowers the devils.

Paw-paw and his ghost-busting hot rod.

Introduction

In John chapter four we read the account of "The woman at the well." Most know the story of how Jesus encountered this woman, battered, bruised and oppressed by the world. A woman forced by life to move from man to man seeking security. Finally she met a man who would forever change her life, Jesus.

As my wife, Tena, often says, it only takes "Just one Touch." (If you have not read her book, "Just One Touch" contact our office for your copy today. It will change your life forever and all those you come in contact with. It takes "Just One Touch.") One touch, one encounter with the anointing and lives are forever changed. Verse 27 says, *"And upon this came his disciples, and marvelled that he talked with the woman..."* Isn't it amazing that we pass by the hurts and pains of this world and are either not affected by it, or, we are too busy to do anything about it. Yes, and even at times marvel when others do what we should or could have done, and yet did not.

The disciples came upon a scene they did not understand. So bound up with tradition and religion they could not operate in the spiritual. Concerned that Jesus was ministering to a woman, who was considered inferior and to make matters worse a Samaritan. A mixed race of people rejected not only by society, but by the Jewish faith.

It appears from verse 27 that Jesus was the "**First on the Scene**." The first to encounter this woman and release the anointing into her life to forever change her.

Such was not the case. Read the beginning of John 4 again. Jesus and his disciples traveled to Samaria. They came to the well together. Jesus chose to sit and rest himself. His disciples walked on into the city to obtain provisions. There were not numerous roads leading into the city, only one from the direction they traveled. A very busy road, a road that led to the community source of water.

1

Notice verse 7, "*there came a woman of Samaria to draw water...*" A woman coming down a dusty road, battered, bruised, oppressed and depressed. Disciples, followers of the living God, anointed and appointed to a day of destiny. Watch! They simply pass each other. I suppose the woman keeps her head down, she knows her place in life. What do you suppose the disciples did? A casual glance, a burning stare, or nothing at all?

There is one sure thing, they were the "**First on the Scene**," yet did nothing. God help us! Help us to be free from tradition, religion, and busyness. Help us to recognize when we are "**First on the Scene**" and release the anointing in our life, to change the lives of those in need.

You are about to embark on a journey. A journey of faith. I wish I could tell you that every time I have seen a need, every time I felt the touch of the Spirit I moved into action, but I can't. You see, I am just like you. A great desire to flow, yet sometimes unable to find the avenue. I believe someone else said the same thing. Paul the apostle made the same confession in Romans chapter seven. Be encouraged, there is hope for us.

This book is a compiling of true life encounters. The dates, times, places, and even names may be vague. Quotation marks may not always seem to be in their proper place, but the encounter and the results are as real today as the day in which it happened.

My prayer is that your faith will explode, as we journey together with those whom God has so gloriously set free. My prayer is that you will move to the next dimension of faith and become sensitive to His touch in such a way that you will recognize your God given opportunities and be fully aware that you are...

FIRST ON THE SCENE!

Where's the Devil?

God has a way of building our faith and showing Himself strong at the same time. I am glad He does not ask us if we desire to be involved, He just places us in the right place at the right time and sits back and watches.

Friday night, First Baptist Church of Stafford, the pastor and five men gather to pray. I am one of the five, freshly returned to God after years of being backslidden. Freshly baptized in the Spirit. Life is good, everything is going great. Don't rock the boat. But God!

The phone rings, the pastor answers it. After a brief moment he returns. "There's a group of people who have encountered a demon possessed woman, they can't get the demon out and want us to come and help." My mind says, "What? Have you lost your mind?" My feet say, "run" but my spirit says, " Be still and know I am God." The pastor then says, "Let's pray and see if we are to go, God will confirm it." I don't know what they were praying, but I prayed, pleeeaaaasssse God don't send us.

After a few moments in prayer a prophecy came forth which in essence said, Go! "Go in my name and I will show you my glory and power." I thought to myself, "shut your mouth," but then I realized it was me doing the speaking. Then I thought, I am going to choke you, shut up! Too late everybody said, "Amen!"

We all got into the car, traveled to Almeda where the people were gathered. As the door opened, I peered over the shoulders of the others, I was the last to go in. Everything seemed normal. Nice home, nice people, refreshments out. "Where's the devil?"

A man and woman come down the hall. Introduced themselves as the homeowner and host. "Where's the devil?" Everyone introduces themselves to each other. "Where's the devil?"

The couple then explained that the demon only manifested at certain times. Lord, don't let it be now. I look into the face of all the others. Is it him? Is it her? "Where's the devil?"

The couple sat down on the sofa and invited me and the others to sit. I sat next to the lady of the house, all the while my mind is saying, "Where's the devil?" My feet are saying, "never mind, run!" My spirit says, "be still and know I am God."

Someone puts on a record of "Amazing Grace." My eyes are darting to and fro around the room. "Where's the devil?" Suddenly I hear a deep gravel demonic voice say, "she's mine." I jerk my head to the side. My God, the lovely lady of the house sitting next to me, her face has changed, it is terrible. My God, it is her the voice is coming from. Feet don't fail me now! In a split second I find myself in a corner behind a pole-lamp praying in tongues like a machine gun. Problem! I have made a mistake. I am in a corner.

The pastor and others begin to command the demon to come out. I am praying "no not now!" Time stands still. I have never seen anything like this before. The woman falls to the floor, slithering like a snake, her tongue is huge, protruding out of her mouth. Where's the door? This thing is not working; they say come out, it says, "No"! Me? I don't care either way, I just want out of this house.

Suddenly a peace that passes all human understanding fills my soul. A power I have never felt comes over me. I step out from behind the lamp, rush to the woman possessed on the floor. With both hands I grab her head, I shout, "Come out in Jesus name!"

Suddenly she drops limp, a smile comes on her face, and peace fills the room. She says, "I am free!"

I found myself on a journey of faith and adventure into the unknown. Prepared by God to be ...

FIRST ON THE SCENE

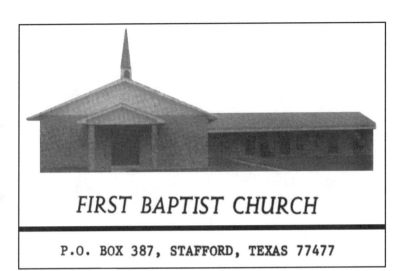

FIRST BAPTIST CHURCH

P.O. BOX 387, STAFFORD, TEXAS 77477

Church and Fellowship Hall

Offering Envelope

Platform

Return Engagement

Never forget, the devil never gives up. Once you have encountered his kingdom and broken his power, he will return for another engagement.

In Luke, chapter 4, when Jesus first encountered the devil himself, He broke his powers with the Word of God. Defeating him on every hand. Yet verse 13 states, *"and when the devil had ended all the temptations, he departed from him for a season"*. As you study the life of Christ you will find that Satan did set up a...

RETURN ENGAGEMENT.

Sunday morning, First Baptist Church of Stafford, God through His people has started a new work. There are five or six couples now baptized in the Holy Spirit, many others are not and are cautiously watching our zeal, wondering what's going on.

I have been asked to sit on the platform with the Pastor to assist him. God is so good, the praise and worship is refreshing, the Word is coming forth in power. The people are receiving the Word.

I wonder who that family is? If that's their son next to them, he sure has a sour look on his face. I bet he wishes he was somewhere else. Excuse me, that's not a sour look, that's a face from hell. Wow, his whole countenance is changing. Oh no, not again. I am just getting over the last encounter. Pleeeaassseee God make him go to sleep. His hands grip the arms of his chair, his face is horrible. Pleeaaassseee don't move or say anything.

Thank God, service is over, no problems. Everyone visits and starts to leave. I am busy closing up. As I step back in the auditorium, I see the Pastor and two other men standing around a chair, it's where the young man was seated. The

Pastor turns and says, "Brother Ford would you come and help us?" Oh God, why didn't I go out the back door?

When I got to where they were, the boy had a death grip on the arms of the chair. The chairs were theater type and bolted to the floor, his feet were pressed against the back of the seat in front of him. His face was a face from hell. His father said, "Son, turn loose of your chair, we need to go home." His son looked into his father's face and said, "I will not leave, you can not make me, he is mine."

Excuse me! Do I know you? Oh brother, it's the Almeda devil, here we go again.

I don't know if I am ready for this. Everyone is trying everything. You would think that four grown men could release the grip of one 15 or 16 year old. Not so, he is glued to the chair. We are sweating like pigs in the noon day sun. How did I get into this? Why me Lord?

After about 30 minutes everyone steps back in exhaustion. His Dad said, "Son, pleeaasseee get up, what's wrong with you?" That deep demonic voice spoke in response, "No, I will never leave, you can't make me, He is mine."

Suddenly a power and strength flooded me. I leaped on top of him, straddled him in the chair like I was riding a horse. I heard myself say, "That's enough, Devil, come out in Jesus name." Yep, it worked again. He fell limp, a smile came on his face, peace filled the place, he accepted Jesus as his Lord and Saviour. Once again, I found myself....

FIRST ON THE SCENE

Congregation on wooden theater type seats

I Begin It -
I Will Complete It

By now my life is like a whirlwind, out of a life of sin into forgiveness. From forgiveness to joy unspeakable. From joy to service in my local church. From service to fullness in the Holy Spirit. Wow, God is good! My family, business and life is moving in a new direction. How could I have been so stupid as not to serve God. But I just have one question, What is this "Devil Chasing" stuff?

Coming from a Baptist background these encounters are almost too much. I mean, get real, let's serve God and leave the Devil and his bunch alone. Yet without a doubt, God is up to something in my life.

I BEGIN IT – I WILL COMPLETE IT

In Philippians 1:6, the Word declares, *"Being confident of this very thing, that he which hath begun a good work in you will perform (complete) it until the day of Jesus Christ."*

Life is a journey of learning; everything, every encounter is a lesson to be learned.

I think of how I was raised in the church. Saved at 9 years old. Knowing what's right and wrong. Yet determined to do my own thing, go my own way. Rebellion with a capital "R". Sin will not only blind you, but will bind you. Not only will it blind you and bind you, it will also make you deaf. Deaf to the voice of God, your Pastor and even your own conscience.

As a young child I had walked to town to obtain a large crate from a hardware store to make a house for my new puppy. In those days, life was easy, slow country living. No problems, just summer time fun.

I had to turn the crate over from side to side to get it to my house. Several of my friends were there but no help, just watching and riding their bikes around me while I flopped and flopped the crate.

"Never stop on the railroad tracks son and never play on the tracks, a train might hit you" my dad would always say. But what does he know! I finally get the crate up the steep incline of the railroad crossing. Boy am I tired! No help, just riding their bikes. Look both ways – no train – listen no sound. Must be everything is OK. That crossing is still in our city, each time I pass by I remember that day as if it were yesterday.

There's a curve in the tracks just before the crossing, in that day there were shotgun shacks on one side for workers and a large wooden water tower on the other, both of which restricted the view in that direction.

WATCH OUT!

Just as I flopped the crate upon the tracks, I heard that sound. The train which traveled in excess of 75 m.p.h. blew its whistle to warn everyone to clear the tracks. What do I do? Leave the crate? Run? Stay? Try to pull it off? What?

WRONG DECISION!

In a split second, I decided to pull the crate one more time to clear the tracks. My friends are yelling, "Ford, get out of the way!" Too late! Just as I grab the crate, I see the largest picture of my life. The front of the train. CRASH! Cardboard, wood, etc. is shattered in a thousand pieces. "Look mom, I can fly like superman!" I am airborne. No pain, everything just a blur. THUD! I hit the bottom of a deep ditch next to the tracks. Whacked out, but alive.

"Richard, Richard, Richard", my dad cried as he ran to where I was. Lifted me up - embraces me with tears in his eyes, "Are you hurt?" No! "Boy, I am going to kill you."

Oh no. Saved from the train, killed by my daddy.

How often does God warn us to get off the tracks of sin? Yet, we just sat there saying, "There's no train coming, I can't see it, nor do I hear it." Watch out! You better get off the track of sin. You may not see nor hear it – but it's coming at killer speed.

Have you ever wondered why sometimes you have such turmoil in your life. Could it be God knocking you off the wrong tracks? Just a thought!

As I reflect back over my life, I realize God has always had His hand on me, keeping me for my appointed time.

Another hot summer day. "Boy, don't ever swim in the canal, you don't know what's in it and the water runs swift." I wish my dad would "get a life", he acts like he knows everything. "Ford, let's go swimming!" Where? In the canal! I can't, Dad told me not to, the water runs too swift. No it don't, they shut the pumps down. Come on, it's hot!

Once again I over-ride my instincts, as well as the instruction of my dad. WOW! The water is cool, still and shallow. Are we having fun or what?

The first one that can dive in and keep their hands to their side will be the champion diver. Look's too shallow! No it's not, just bend your body when you hit the water, you'll break shallow.

No one seems to be able to do it, everyone chickening out at the last moment. No sweat, I thrive on challenges, get out of my way and let Tarzan through.

Standing on the old wooden bridge, I climb up on the top side rail. Ford, don't dive from there, get down on the side. Shut up! You don't know nothing, you can't ever do it.

Tarzan leaves his launching pad. Am I great or what? Gliding through the air, arms pinned to my side, I pierce the water like a bullet. WOW! I did it, I am the ..... THUD!

My head hits bottom. Darkness envelops me, then suddenly lights. The brightest light I have ever seen totally surrounds me, peace, calmness, stillness like I have never known envelops me. I am suspended in time and space. I feel like I am floating in another dimension, no pain, just peace. WOW, I've never seen anything like this before. I have no knowledge of what's happened, who I am, where I am, nothing but this glimpse of time within time.

Suddenly, I am jerked back to reality, my two friends pull me out of the water upon the bank. Ford, are you alive? I don't know, what happened?

You darn fool, we told you not to dive from the top, you hit bottom. How do you know I hit bottom? Look at you, your head is packed in mud to your ears.

Hey, something is wrong, I can't move. Boy, your daddy is going to kill us. Slowly, I recover, my neck will swell, and become stiff for days.

Mrs. Ford, Richard hurt himself. "Oh sweety, what happened?" I hit my head on the bottom of the canal when I dove in, I almost broke my neck, I almost drowned, but Mommy, I saw a great light, it's like time stood still, it's like I could breathe under water, it's like .... "Richard Frank, I am going to beat you to death, boy." Oh no, saved from death by the Angels, only to live so Mommy can kill me.

What did I learn through those encounters. Looking back, I would have to say, "Stop – Look – Listen in life or it could cost you your life." I would have to say, "All day, all night, Angels watching over me". I would have to say, "He which has begun a good work in you, will complete it."

Oh and just one more thing, I wish on those days, I had not been ...

FIRST ON THE SCENE

R/R Crossing

The curve. Tower was on the left.
Worker shack on the right.

The launching pad.

The landing strip (ditch).

Wooden bridge has been replaced.
Launching pad.

Landing strip (bottom).

Crispy Critter

Like I was saying, God has unusual ways to develop our faith in preparing us for His plan.

Little did I know that the encounters in life and with all these devil's were just the beginning. God preparing me for my life's mission. Busting devils and setting people free. I guess He knows how much I enjoyed fighting in the natural and living on the cutting edge when I was in the world.

As my journey with God continued, I noticed resistance building around me. At times it seemed that if things could go wrong, they would. What happened to all the new found joy? It's still there, but now you have a new enemy. The one you used to serve is now trying to stop you. The one you used to serve is now trying to cut you down. Why? When you gave your life to Jesus and decided to serve God, you became a threat to the devil and a thorn in his _ _ _ _.

God was determined to develop me into a powerhouse for Him. Devil busting, demon stomping child of God. Storming Hell with a squirt gun. With my "Red-Hot Christian" cap on and my "No Fear" t-shirt flapping in the wind. Plundering hell and populating heaven.

But He had to show me quickly how we have power over all the power of the enemy (Luke 10: 18-19). "That greater is He that is in us than he that is in the world" (I John 4:4) "How we are strong and the Word of God lives in us and we have overcome that wicked one" (I John 2:14). "How the weapons of our warfare are not carnal, but mighty through God to pulling down strongholds" (II Cor. 10:4). And that we must have on the armor of God as we move into enemy territory (Eph. 6:10-18). Fully understanding we are called – anointed and appointed to set the captives free (Luke 4:18-19) and never forgetting we can do nothing in our own strength (Zech. 4:6).

CRISPY CRITTER

Saturday afternoon, cutting my yard; boy, I wish these ants would find another place to build their house. When they bite you, they bite you. There's something inside me that just cannot stand to be controlled by the lower creation. Ants all over my bare feet, chewing until their little belly is full. All the time I am saying, "You want some of me?" (Please don't ever do what I did. It's too dangerous! It's really stupid!)

OK! Enough is enough, where's my gas can? Here, have a drink of this you little demon possessed ants. Die! WOW, look at them curl up.

Continuing mowing; WOW! What was that? A huge snake in the ditch shoots by my feet. In a split second I am 20 feet away. Where did he go? Cautiously looking, must be in the driveway culvert. Stay back as far as you can. Peep into the culvert. WOW! There he is, right in the middle, coiled up in a fighting position. My heart is pumping wide open. Never did like snakes, you just can't trust them.

What to do? I know, I saw this on T.V. when people wanted to catch rattle snakes. Toss a little gas, the fumes will run him out, then I will chop his little head off.

In goes the gas, I smile, I wait. Nothing! I peep into the pipe. WOW! Still there, looks a little madder than before. Must not have reached him. The wind must have blown the fumes out the other end. No problem, toss a little more gas in from the other end. Never give up, just look for another way. Take that you slithering devil from hell. Wait, wait; now peep in. WOW! Still coiled up and now seriously mad at me. I think he wants out, but I keep looking in. Oh, brilliant idea. Toss a match in and set fire to the gas that will bring him out. Right? Wrong!

Boom! I leap backwards, the earth shakes, fire shoots out both ends of the culvert like a cannon. My heart is pounding so fast I think it's heart attack city.

The smoke clears, wow, what have I done? Where's that snake? Tena runs out, "What in the world was that? What's happening?" Get back woman, this is man's work. I am at war!

Cautiously I peep into the pipe. Unbelievable! The snake is still in a coiled, striking position. Now wait a minute! Uh oh, something is different. No movement. WOW! It's a **crispy critter!** A well done snake. I win!

THE MORAL?

Never play with matches! Never play with gas! Never mix the two! It's insane! It's stupid!

THE MORAL?

"Is not my word like as a fire? saith the Lord; and like a hammer that breaketh the rock in pieces?" (Jer. 23:29) *"Thou art my battle axe and weapons of war: for with thee will I break in pieces the nations, and with thee will I destroy kingdoms."* (Jer. 51:20)

I SEE IT!

Just as we have authority over the lower animal kingdom, we also have authority over the lower kingdom of the devil (Luke 10:18- 19). WOW! *". . . when the enemy shall come in, like a flood the Lord will lift up a standard against him."* (Isaiah 59:19) WOW! *"The Lord shall cause thine enemies that rise up against thee to be smitten before thy face: They shall come out against thee one way, and flee before thee seven ways."* (Deut. 28:7) *" And the Lord shall make thee the head, and not the tail; and thou shalt be above only, and thou shalt not be beneath; if that thou hearken unto the commandments of the Lord thy God, which I command thee this day, to observe and to do them:"* (Deut. 28: 13) WOW!

I SEE IT!

Nothing can stop a submitted, obedient, Word filled, faith acting child of God. Devil! You want some of me? Oh, by the way, remember to use wisdom when you are...

FIRST ON THE SCENE

Don't you wish it was this simple.
Forget the belly, focus on the devil!

Moving On In The Spirit
A Believing Unbeliever

Wow! Two demon's down, notches in my gun, gun smoking (but not from gas). No turning back! No turning around! When you realize how big God is in you, when you realize how big you are in God, the devil has a problem. Little sister-in-law you need to be saved. "Not now I am having too much fun."

One evening the phone rings. "Hello, this is Debra. My boyfriend has devils in him, can I bring him over? Will ya'll pray for him? I know if ya'll pray, he will be alright." An unbeliever, believing in the power of God, wow! "Come on over."

We open the door, there's Debra with her boyfriend. Nice looking guy. You're doing better Debra, I see you have come out of the junk yard to find your boyfriends!

They sit down and he begins to share how he has been fooling around in the occult, Ouija board, etc. Now, voices in the night, now, terror in the day. Trouble on every hand. Know this, you can not play in the devil's yard and come out untouched.

We shared the gospel with them both. Why not just cast the devil out and move on? No way! The devil will only come back, find the house empty and return with seven demons more powerful than himself. (Matthew 12:43-45)

"Debra, wait in the other room," "Why?" "The devil is about to manifest." Hey! Where's Debra? In the other room!

Tena and I begin to pray, bringing the glory of God into the room. Suddenly, his face turns sour and his voice changes. Deep voices begin to speak.

Excuse me! Do I know you? Yes I do, you demon from hell, I met you in Almeda. Come out in Jesus name!

A loud scream, the boy falls limp, a smile comes on his face, and peace fills the room. Jesus is there, salvation is there. He is born-again. Debra, you need to get saved! Not now I am having too much fun. Debra is going to have to find a new boyfriend, the party is over. Why?...

FIRST ON THE SCENE

Debra Alderman

I am too young to be making decisions. I'll just go for a boat ride.

Hey, I got the next dance.

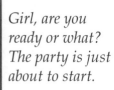

Girl, are you ready or what? The party is just about to start.

Show Down or Hoe-Down?

My life is changing so fast I can't keep up with it. When Jesus touches you, He will "fire" you and when He "fires" you, your destiny is established.

As God begins to change me, there seems to be a stirring inside of me. I began to feel uncomfortable. What is this?

Before committing my life back to the Lord, I had begun to search for something good. I was not interested in church, in fact I was turned off by what I had seen, people in our city who said they loved God, but lived a lifestyle of the opposite. I realize it was just another excuse, but, hey, I needed an excuse to run from God.

I ran into a trap set by the devil, "The Masonic Lodge." An organization designed to draw you into bondage. An organization that held me captive for six years. (For a complete exposure of the Masonic Lodge and my involvement, obtain my book "Set Free." In this book I reveal everything about the Masonic Lodge that you ever wanted to know, but no one dared to tell – I tell it all.)

If we intend to serve God, if we intend to be used of God, if we intend to set others free, then we ourselves must be set free.

COME OUT!

Suddenly the truth of the Masonic Lodge is revealed to me. My eyes were opened because my heart was opened.

My God, how could I have been so deceived? Why did I not see the shallowness of this organization? Simple, flesh ruled instead of Spirit led!

The Lodge proclaims it takes you "from darkness to light," yet, the opposite is true. The Masonic Lodge takes you deeper into darkness than you could ever imagine. Good people? Yes! But blinded to the truth.

23

NOW I SEE!

Never is the name of Jesus used in the Lodge. A system of good works is taught. Involvement with unbelievers of every walk of life is taught. Fellowship with God haters, Christ rejectors is encouraged. The whole system of the Masonic order is rooted in ancient cult worship. Blood binding oaths required of each person.

COME OUT!

"Then said Jesus to those Jews which believed on him, If ye continue in my word, then are ye my diciples indeed: And ye shall know the truth, and the truth shall make you free. If the Son therefore shall make you free, ye shall be free indeed." John 8: 31-32, 36. I walked away from Masonry, focusing my efforts toward God and serving the local church. Now God begins to use me in a new and dramatic way. Little did I know that a "show down" was coming.

God had begun to send men by my store that was interested in the lodge. They all ask, "Why did you get out?" I always took the opportunity to share, even giving them literature to study to show that Masonry was incompatable with the Word of God.

SHOW DOWN!

Little did I realize the turmoil I had been causing in the Lodge as I was speaking out against the order. Masonic charges were filed against me. "Conduct unbecoming a Mason."

WOW! These guys are serious. A trial? Yes a trial! For the first time in the history of Sugarland Lodge #1141, a member had charges filed against him, and to make matters worse an ex-officer. "Past Worshipful Master."

My mind stirred with the possibilities of that day. The blood binding oath I took. Was this for real? The embarassment that would be felt that day. The rejection, shame, ridicule, etc. so I made up my mind, that day would not be a "show down" but a ...

HOE-DOWN!

Saturday morning, I am nervous as a cat. When I arrived at the Lodge it was overflowing with Lodge members that had come to witness this historic event.

Was I alone? Not on your life! Not only was God with me, but over 50 members of the church had come to support me, waiting outside, interceding for me.

The devil was looking for a show down to shut me down, but what he got was a hoe-down.

After the charges were read and I was asked to respond as to whether I was guilty or not, I responded, guilty! Thank God I am guilty! Guilty of spreading the gospel of Jesus Christ! Guilty of taking people from darkness to light, from bondage to freedom. Guilty? Yes!

I stood to address those assembled to judge me. Once again the sweet presence of the Lord filled my life as I stood before these men, once again the power of God rose up inside of me.

With one bold step I took over the meeting. Shutting the devil's plans down. For approximately 45 minutes, I proclaimed the truth of God's Word, destroying the myth of Masonry. Boldness building with every minute. **Show Down**? No way, it was a **Hoe-Down** as I danced on the devil's head that day.

When that day ended, victory was mine. Expelled from the Masonic order, but free.

Oh, something else happened. My name was recorded in Hell, (Acts 19:55). That day I had turned hell upside down, the city was in an uproar. Tormenting hell would become my life's work. Being a pestilent fellow would become my trade mark, (Acts 24:5).

25

There was another important lesson learned, if you are going to keep crying "Come out," you yourself will have to "Come out" or you cannot be...

FIRST ON THE SCENE

NOTICE OF ELECTION

(To Candidate)

Sugar Land , Texas, March 16 , 19 71

To Mr. Richard Frank Ford

Dear Sir:

I have the pleasure to inform you that at a Stated Communication of

Sugar Land Lodge No. 1141 , A. F. & A. M., held March 15, 19 71,

you were elected to receive the Mysteries of Masonry in this Lodge.

Please present yourself for initiation on Monday evening

April 12 , 19 71, at 8:00 P. M. o'clock.

Respectfully yours,

Andrew U. Blair Secretary.

(SEAL)

Andrew V. Blair, Sec.

Form No. 47—5M—10-65—Masonic Home Press.

Notice of Suspension or Expulsion for Un-Masonic Conduct

Hall of SUGAR LAND Lodge No. 1141 , A. F. & A. M.

SUGAR LAND , Texas, February 17 , 19 79

To Richard Frank Ford
2701 Charles Ln.
, Sugar Land, Texas

Dear Sir:

You are hereby notified that at a trial held before a Trial Commission on February 17 ,
19 79 you were (expelled) (suspended) for conduct unbecoming a Mason.

By Order of the Lodge.

(Seal)

Andrew U. Blair

Buddy Blair Secretary.

Form No. 13—100—3-72 Masonic Home Press

27

Control Yourself

Galatians, chapter 5, verses 22-25 declare the fruit of the spirit. The same chapter also declares the works of the flesh. No problem, the flesh is out of the junk yard, I am now serving God.

Little did I know what God was about to do. I was set up to see how weak in character (God's character) I was. Saved? Yes! Baptized in water and Spirit? Yes! Love God? Yes! Serving God? Yes! Yet something more is needed. What? Godly character – Fruits of the Spirit.

CONTROL YOURSELF

1:00 a.m. the phone rings in my home. Now who could that be? Somebody broke down, needing auto parts?

"Hello!" "Brother Ford, I hate to call so late." My mind says, "Liar, if you hate it, don't do it." Now watch this. I said, "That's OK, no problem." Liar, tell the truth.

"Brother Ford my wife and I are having hell. Can you help us?" "How long you been fighting?" "Three months!" "Three months? And you decided to call me at 1:00 a.m. - Listen this is not the time for this." "But Brother Ford, I don't know what to do, I feel like taking my belt off and spanking her." "Look, I don't care what you do. Just try not to call me this early in the morning. I'll talk to you at church, good-by."

3:00 a.m. the phone rings. My eyes are burning, my mind is fuzzy. Not again! "Brother Ford, you've got to help me!" "Now what?" "I did it!" "You did what?" "I took my belt and tried to whip her." "You what?" "Well, you said, do whatever I felt like doing." "What happened?" "She went crazy, Brother Ford, she went outside and ripped my rear view mirror off the car and beat the windows out of my car. Brother Ford, I believe the little lady has devils in her."

Oh God, I am not ready for this!

CONTROL YOURSELF

What a week, I got through the last episode. The car's a wreck but they're still together. Boy, people are crazy.

Friday night, 3:00 a.m. The phone rings. Oh no, not again. "Hello!" "Brother Ford we need your help." Another couple having hell at 3:00 a.m. Whatever happened to four in the afternoon? "Well, what do you want me to do about it?" "Help me Brother Ford! She broke a lamp and some dishes." "Look, I am worn out from this whole week! All I've had is hell." "Brother Ford, what should I do?" "I don't care, at 3:00 in the morning, do whatever you want to." Click! Give me a break, I hope they tear up the whole house.

CONTROL YOURSELF

7:00 a.m. warm cup of coffee, after this week I am going to need several gallons. The phone rings, Tena answers it, I've had all the phone calls I need. "It's for you darling!" "Good God woman, darling has had all the phone calls he wants for the next two years!" "Hello!" "Brother Ford it's _____." Oh brother, last night's nut. "Yea, what do you want?" "I just wanted to tell you that me and _____ are so happy this morning, it's unbelievable how we feel." "Really! How did that happen?" (I sure didn't do anything.) "It's you Brother Ford, you did it." "What? I did what?" "You told me to just do whatever I felt like doing, so we began to bust up everything." "Everything?" "Yes, we broke every dish, every lamp, every piece of furniture." "What?" "Oh, that's not all we beat holes in the sheetrock of every room. We've totally destroyed our home, I bet there's $20,000.00 worth of damage." "Oh my God man!" "It's OK Brother Ford, thank you. We have nothing left but each other, it's wonderful."

CONTROL YOURSELF

Oh, God, what have I done. What's going on. "Richard, if you are going to be used of Me you must allow My character to come through you. I am in the people business. They need strong leadership. Don't look at this as an infringement into your life. I will teach you how to control yourself and the situations of life that you encounter. But you must remember, let them see Me, not you."

WOW! God is good, the lessons continue and He still desires to use us in spite of ourselves. All we have to remember is let God shine through when we are ...

FIRST ON THE SCENE

Who Said What?

The phone rings. It is the believing, unbeliever, Debra. "Hi ya'll, my boyfriend down at the liquor store has had a bad motorcycle accident, they say he will never walk again. Will ya'll go pray for him?" Sure!

Tena and I make our way to the hospital. Wow! What a tragedy. Battered, bruised, and bandaged from head to toe. "Hi, Debra asked us to come, can we pray for you?" A weak nod, yes.

WHO SAID WHAT?

You may never walk again, you may have brain damage, you... No! No! Jesus said, you shall live and not die to declare the works of God. Jesus said, by my stripes you were and are healed.

The gospel comes forth, his eyes fill with tears, and he receives Jesus. Healing is released. Debra loses another boyfriend, and hell loses a liquor salesman. Why? We were...

FIRST ON THE SCENE

Watch Out!

Serving God and owning your own business is a challenge, especially if you yourself was once the servant of sin. But I made the switch from darkness to light. God is blessing my family and business like I could have never imagined.

The front door of the auto parts store flies open. "Somebody call an ambulance, some guy is having a fit." I shot out the front door as if a rocket had gone off in my shoes. People have come from the drive-in store next door, standing around looking, and holding their beer.

Without hesitation, I drop down beside the man. I lift his head and look into his face. Teeth clinched, eyes rolled back into his head, and foam coming out of his mouth. Excuse me! Do I know you? Yep, it is that same old devil from Almeda. "You foul devil, loose him and let him go. Come out in Jesus name." Yes, you guessed it. His body fell limp, peace came all over him.

I look around, where did everybody go? Oh, I remember, when I shouted in Jesus' name, somebody shouted "watch out." All the heathens ran back by the store. Why? Once again...

FIRST ON THE SCENE

I Am Ready!
Look Out!

I've discovered in my walk with God that my greatest enemy is not the devil, but myself. Don't misunderstand me, I am not diminishing the power of the devil, but all it takes is the Name and the power of the Name to drive him out. But what about ourselves. Ever try to cast yourself out? Won't work.

By now I believe I am surely God's gift to Stafford if not to the whole world.

I AM READY!

Look out! Proverbs 16: 18-19, "*Pride goeth before destruction, and an haughty spirit before a fall. Better it is to be of an humble spirit with the lowly, than to divide the spoil with the proud.*"

One of the dangers of being used of God is we believe we are something special. But Romans 12:3 warns, "*...not to think of himself more highly than he ought to think; but to think soberly according as God hath dealt to every man the measure of faith.*"

I begin to share with my wife that God surely had great things in store for us and it would not surprise me what He would do. Just look how he is using us. Serving in the local church, nursing home, hospitals, etc. I mean the sky is the limit.

I AM READY!

God send us all the people that need help. I am ready! One by one, two by two's, they began to come. Day and night, phone ringing, visiting my home, my auto parts store.

STOP!

I can't take anymore. I am losing my mind. Let them all go to hell, I am out of here. Enough is enough! But, I thought you said you were ready. Forget what I said, I am out of here.

I rented a large drive around fully equipped travel camper, not only drive it, sleep in it, cook in it, restroom, t.v., the whole works.

My nerves are shot, my brain is fried. The Fruits of the Spirit have fallen off the tree to rot on the ground. Compassion, pity? What's that! Just get out of town!

Buckle the pickup truck behind. "Tena, kids, shut up! Get in the camper. Sit down and be quiet." "Darling is everything hooked up right, we don't want any problems with the truck being pulled." Darling said, "Shut up, woman. This is man's work. What do you know?" The kids? They don't say nothing. The mad man from Gadara is back.

We're out of here! But I thought you said, "I am ready!" Forget it! We've made it to the Katy Freeway. Total silence inside. Why? The mad man from Gadara is back.

Now what? Something is wrong, it feels like I am pulling 500 tons. Just what I need. I pull over, start checking out everything. A pretty little head looks out the window, "Is everything OK darling." "No! Darling forgot to secure the steering wheel of the pickup. I've just about pulled the rubber off both front tires. Shut up, get back inside."

We're out of here! Pulling nicely now. "Sweety, why don't you boil some sausage on the stove, kids give me a coke." Daddy's back!

Twenty minutes later, no sausage, inside the camper is burning up from the heat of the stove. "My God, can't anyone do anything right?" The mad man from Gadara is back. "Everybody just sit down and shut up and don't move. I think I am losing my mind." Think? It looks like a sure thing.

My emotions are shot. I find myself acting like every other nut in the world. What's that? Oh brother, Tena's praying in tongues behind me. I think I will tell her to shut up, it's not the right time. No, better not, God could knock me out of the camper doing 50 m.p.h..

Suddenly, sweet peace enters, calmness is flooding us. I think I am going to live. Sorrow fills my heart. "I'm sorry for acting like a nut, forgive me." Daddy's back!

God, what's happening? Did one of those devils jump on me? "No, you needed a lesson on compassion and pride. You lost your sensitivity to the needs of the people and were operating in your own strength. I just wanted to show you, you're not as ready as you thought."

WOW! God is so good, He just keeps on developing us despite our weaknesses.

Remember, compassion must always precede action when you're...

FIRST ON THE SCENE

Mommy, I don't see Daddy anywhere, come on out.

Natalie

It wasn't our fault he dragged the truck 50 miles side ways.

Mike & Donnie

O' great, he wants to sell me a truck with both front wheels half gone.

Mike

Construction Devil

Our life, the apostle Paul said, is like a letter, like a book. As we look back over our life, we can see how God will involve us in His business, in order to train and develop us for the next step to our Divine destiny.

Wow! Are we growing in God? Encounter after encounter causing us to grow in leaps and bounds. Why is God using me so strongly? It is certainly not my abilities, **it must be my availability.**

The church needs a Sunday School wing added to the present building. My background positions me to design and oversee the project. What a joy and thrill, to once again get to do something for God, and such an important task. To oversee the construction of a place where hundreds of children and adults will be taught the ways of God.

The phone rings at my auto parts store. "Mr. Ford, this is Mr. _____. Twice this week I have found a drunk sleeping in the new wing we are constructing." Without a second of thought I respond, "Run him off and if he comes back tell me and I'll have him arrested." Does that sound like wisdom and compassion or what?

But God! After hanging up the phone I begin to feel convicted over my response. I drove to the church in hopes of finding the drunk. He is nowhere to be found. Boy, did I miss it. I could have at least tried to get him saved.

Two days later I am compelled to go to the church. I don't know why; I know there is no construction being done that day. When I drive up, I see a man sitting under the porch of the new wing that is under construction.

I walk up and ask, "May I help you?" He leaps to his feet only to stagger back. It is the drunk!

I immediately move toward him. He is not sure who I am or what I am about to do. I explain the need for him not to hang around the church for his safety and the concern for others.

He staggers back and responds, "Ya'll are all alike. Nobody cares about anyone anymore." I realize he is just about right. It seems I am more concerned for the natural than for the eternal. I switch over. "Do you know Jesus? Does He live in your heart?" I was not prepared for his next statement. "That's it! That's the one I am looking for. Who is this Jesus?"

Suddenly, the power and glory of God descended like a cloud. The drunk looks at me with astonishment. I know he saw Christ in me, the Hope.

For the next two hours, I shared Jesus from Genesis to Revelation. We moved from room to room, as he would back up. But God was in pursuit. Where can we go to get away from God? What God pursues, He overtakes!

As I look back, it reminds me of the story in Luke chapter 24 about the two men from Emmaus who encountered Jesus after the resurrection. They said their hearts burned within them. This drunk was on fire. Fire from heaven that cannot be quenched.

DECISION TIME!

We found ourselves in one of the back rooms. Time is over. It is decision time. "Do you want Jesus to come and change your life?" You see I discovered this man was a college professor from New York. Drinking had cost him his family, career, everything he had. He hesitated, "I just don't know if this would work, I can't leave the bottle alone." Before I knew what I was saying I said, "If God does not sober you up right now and change your life, I'll drive you down the street and the booze is on me."

With astonishment he looked at me and said, "I think you mean business." I responded, "I do! Jesus is either Lord or He is not. He will do what He said or He won't. If He doesn't then I am out of here."

He fell to his knees in the saw dust. I fell beside him, the sweet anointing came. I laid hands on him commanding the devil to loose him, for the alcohol to leave his body, for Jesus to sober him and save him. Suddenly he leaped to his feet shouting, "I am sober, I am sober, I can think clearly." Jesus showed up! We prayed some more, I gave him some money for food and bus fare back to New York.

He left for the bus station, which was a few blocks from us. I turned to walk back through the building to my car, there was Mr. ____ (the builder) standing there. He said, "I have never seen anything like that in all my life." Little did I know but he had come upon us and witnessed the entire scene. That day a construction devil was driven out, and a contractor which was Church of Christ, saw the power of Pentecost. Why?...

FIRST ON THE SCENE

Construction site

View of new wing

Party's Over

The phone rings. "Hello!" "Hi, this is Debra, can I come over I got a new car." "Sure come on over." Later this little green car drives up. Oh! Excuse me, do I know you. Nope, my mistake. It is just Debra's new car, a Dodge Demon. Can you believe a little green car with a picture of a little red devil holding a pitch fork on the side. Debra, you don't need this car and you need to get saved. Nope, I am having too much fun.

PARTY'S OVER!

After months of intercession, after many encounters with God, the phone rings. "Hello, this is Debra, can I come over?" Sure come on over. The door opens, Debra falls in, covered with the stench of sin and the world. "I need to get saved." Tena tells her, "Debra this is not a game. If you don't mean business, I will not pray for you, if you won't serve God, I will not pray for you."

PRAY!

Debra is gloriously saved. Drives off, rounds the corner, the Holy Ghost fills her to overflowing. The devil is mad. Why? We were...

FIRST ON THE SCENE

See I'm saved. Look at my cross t-shirt.

Debra Alderman is founder of Debra Alderman Ministries
traveling all over the world setting the captives free.

Mad Devil

When God starts blessing, the devil starts messing. Tena and I both have grown. We have heard the voice of the Lord say, "Who will go for us, who can we send?" We have responded, "Here am I Lord, send me!"

My wife's faith is so wild, she begins to pray for cocker spaniel dogs. Guess what, dogs came from everywhere. Three cockers at one time.

Three a.m. one of the dogs begins to bark. Not just bark, but bark, and bark. You know the feeling, you love your dog but not at 3:00 a.m. I'd go to the door and shout, shut up! No good, he barks and barks. That's it. He's dead. Out of bed, outside still in my underwear. (Country living and no neighbors close by.) Tena behind me, "Don't you kill my dog, God gave me that dog!" My response, "I am going to send that dog to dog heaven."

When I stepped out of the house, the dog was running back and forth next to an unmowed pasture, hair bristled on his back, teeth snarled, barking and barking. What's wrong with that dog, is it going nuts? Suddenly, the hair on the back of my neck and arms stands out. Uh-oh, excuse me, do I know you? Yep, the devil from Almeda, but this time he brought help. God opened our eyes. Whether it was in the natural or supernatural, I don't know. I do know I saw huge, black demonic figures moving back and forth next to our property. We are talking mad devils. Then, just as suddenly, huge angels appeared on the edge inside our property. Arms folded, and sword in hand. Wow! Angels watching over me! Hey you, yeah you devil, you want some of me? What's going on? Mad devil! Why...

FIRST ON THE SCENE

Dogs, dogs and more dogs. I guess Tena has dog faith.

I Am Well Pleased

You don't have to search for something to do for God. Just get involved in kingdom business. People will beat a path to your door. They are hurting and looking for just one touch.

The phone rings. "Hello, this is _____ and _____ we've got real problems. _____ can't sleep. She is full of fear and anxieties. Can we come over?" "Sure come on over."

We open the door. Wow! Is this the lady we know? Eyes full of terror. "What's happened?" "We don't know, somehow the devil has found a way in and is tormenting her." After a time of ministry of the Word, it is time to pray. I lay hands on her and begin to pray the promises of God. Suddenly, a blood curdling scream comes from her mouth. Uh-oh! Excuse me, do I know you?

You foul spirit of fear, come out in Jesus name. Peace, joy, and contentment filled her life. They leave, we are ready for bed. It is 2:00 a.m. We start closing down the house. Music? Must be one of the kids' radios. Not in Natalie's room. Not in Mike and Donnie's room. Oh, must be our clock radio. No, not in our room. Where is it coming from?

Must be the A/C pulling air through the return vent in the hall. No! Where is it coming from? I meet my wife in the den, we are both looking around. Suddenly, God speaks. "It is my angels, the choir of heaven. They are singing for you and to you. I am well pleased." Why?...

FIRST ON THE SCENE

Toothless Wonder

Jesus had marvelous ways to build the faith of His disciples by using natural illustrations to teach supernatural principles. One such example is found in Mark, chapter four, when Jesus said that a farmer sowed seed. Then He went on to describe where the seed fell and the results of the sowing. As He shared this familiar story of the farmer, He then began to relate it to the supernatural principles.

As my journey continued with God, I found the Lord would periodically cause a real life encounter to be used to encourage and instruct me in my walk in the Spirit.

TOOTHLESS WONDER

In the auto parts business every day was an adventure. Never knowing from day to day what would be encountered. It seemed as if I was forever hiring young men and giving them a chance to become something in life. I suppose it was God's way of training me for my mission in life. I realize that reaching out and changing lives has always been a part of my life.

"Johnny, deliver these parts over to _____ Gulf, they're waiting for them and watch out for that dog. I wish they would do something about that dog. I know they need him at night to keep everything secured, but they need to put him up during the day before he bites someone."

One 250 lb. Saint Bernard, ugly and slobbering all over everything. The owner keeps telling us "He won't hurt you." Whenever I or one of my men would drive up, we never got out until we made sure the dog was chained or out of the way. Today we're under a lot of pressure, everyone wanted everything yesterday. Hurry, hurry, hurry.

Johnny pulls into the driveway, his mind is on getting there and getting back. He forgot the dog! As he stepped out of the pickup and hurried to the work bay, out of the corner of his eye he saw the dog lunging at him. Before he could think what to do or make any type of movement to safety, the dog grabbed the thigh of his leg with his mouth. Johnny screamed in horror, his heart skipped a beat, his mind says "do something!" Too late, the dog is on him like a light, with his jaws clamped on his thigh. Fear and horror gripping him.

While Johnny is fighting for his life, his screams fill the air, his body twisting about, everyone is laughing. Laughing? Why? They knew something we didn't know. This dog had no teeth. For two years this dog had ruled the world, we walked in fear, controlled by his appearance.

TOOTHLESS WONDER

The devil is the same way, keeping us at bay while he walks about us as a roaring lion. Making us believe he will destroy us and all the while, Jesus has pulled his teeth. Isaiah, chapter 14, verse 16 says we will one day look upon the devil and say, "*. . . is this the man that made the earth to tremble, that did shake kingdoms;*" This toothless wonder did all of that?

When Johnny came back and began to share what happened, we all laughed at ourselves and him. I know he was telling the truth. How? There was a great big wet spot on his thigh coated with slobber.

Remember don't worry about the toothless wonder, just be...

FIRST ON THE SCENE

Ford Auto Supply

The Fearless Duo.
Richard & Johnny

Blissful Ignorance

Remember, how I said that God sometimes does not ask us if we want to be involved, He just puts us in the right place at the right time and then sits back and watches.

The phone at the auto parts store rings. "Mr. Ford, this is Terry's wife. Terry has had a nervous breakdown and is addicted to drugs. They have him in the county hospital, can you go pray for him?" "Sure, I'll go."

I step into the hospital, seems strange, it is not like most hospitals, must be because of the type of treatment. Mental and addiction.

The lady at the information desk said he is on the fifth floor. I go to the elevator. Press the button, nothing happens. What is wrong? A malfunction maybe. I keep pressing the button and wait. Finally the door opens a doctor steps out and I step in, the door closes. I press number five, nothing happens. I wait, what's wrong? Suddenly, up we go, the elevator stops. The door won't open. I press, I punch, I kick. Nothing happens. Time stands still. Movement, thank God I thought I was stuck. Hey, I am going down again. Two nurses step in and press five, the door opens. I step out with them. Where is Terry? I see him in a ward with a lot of others. The gospel comes forth, I pray, he is saved and delivered. "How did you get up here" he said. "I rode the elevator." "Yeah but this is a lockup ward nobody can get in but officials." "Well, that is me. An official representative for Jesus. Gotta go, see you later." I push the elevator button, nothing happens. Suddenly the door opens a man steps out, I step in. Nothing happens. I wait, I pray. The elevator goes down, the door opens somebody steps in and I step out.

I found out that this type of elevator is a security elevator. You must have a key for it to work. Why did it work for me? I have been given the keys to the kingdom. That is why I am...

FIRST ON THE SCENE

The Battle Rages On

In Luke, chapter 10, Jesus reveals a powerful truth. In eternity past, a war erupted in heaven. Lucifer the anointed cherub rose up in rebellion against God. According to Ezekiel 28: 13-17, lucifer was anointed and appointed by God to a position of leadership over the angelic host. And according to Isaiah 14: 12-15, pride entered his heart, the desire to be like God filled his mind, rebellion exploded into war.

Jesus was there! Luke 10: 18 "... *I beheld Satan as lightning fall from heaven.*" Lucifer and his army of rebellion was cast from heaven; now called satan, devil, deceiver, his army referred to as demons.

Daniel, chapter 10, confirms the war that began in eternity past and rages on into this present age. Daniel had set his heart to hear from God. Fasting and prayer became his avenue to God. An angelic being appears to Daniel declaring that God had heard his prayers and he was sent to Daniel from God with the answer. Watch this, verse 13, "*But the prince of the kingdom of Persia withstood me one and twenty days: but, lo, Michael, one of the Chief Princes, came to help me...*" WOW! War in the heavenlies!

Paul confirmed our warfare in Eph. 6:10-18. Forces sent from satan to delay, detour and stop the child of God from reaching his destiny.

From eternity past until eternity future, there will be war. Revelation 20 reveals the final outcome of satan and his hosts of demons when Michael, the waring angel, once again is dispatched by God to pull him down for the final count.

THE BATTLE RAGES ON

God has been using me in a way that almost seems like a dream. Encounter after encounter, pulling down strongholds, breaking the power of the devil off of lives. Little did I know, God was preparing me for fulltime service for Him. Building Godly character, teaching me how to trust in Him, listening to that still small voice and obeying without hesitation. Showing me the power that was within me. Demonstration after demonstration of His Majesty, Glory and Power.

There was yet another lesson that had not quite been learned. The lesson?

THE BATTLE RAGES ON

One afternoon, in the latter part of September of 1978, 21 months prior to God calling me into fulltime service to Him as Pastor of "Family Worship Center," the phone rings. It's some girls and boys who are in 4-H. I'd always told them that if I could ever help them to be sure to call me. On this particular day, they wanted me to come to help prepare their lambs for the Fort Bend County Fair. I, of course, told them I would come. My children raised lambs, and when it came time to show the animals, you had to get them ready. You must wash them and fleece their wool so that it is as white as snow; then you shear them using a piece of equipment called lamb shears. They are very sharp and very dangerous and require great care in their use.

I had already finished the whole morning of shearing lambs out in the country for these kids. We had come home. My children had three lambs and some finishing touches needed to be done. I had already completed two and was on the third lamb.

I had the clippers in my hand. My son, Donnie, was holding the lamb. It was as if someone grabbed the clippers and jammed them into my arm, literally ripping the flesh open between the elbow and the hand. I knew that I was in trouble. I cried out "Oh, my God." I dropped the clippers on the ground, I yelled at my son to put the lamb in the pen and to turn the clippers off, that I had to get to the hospital. My whole hand went completely numb, and blood gushed forth out of my arm like I have never experienced before or had ever seen in my life. **Life is in the blood.**

All through the pages of God's Word the blood has been the ultimate sacrifice for sin. The first Scriptural accounting of blood was in the Garden when God cast man from the Garden because of his disobedience and his rebelling against God.

Gen. 3:21-24 *"Unto Adam also and to his wife did the Lord God make coats of skins and clothed them. And the Lord God said, Behold, the man is become as one of us, to know good and evil: and now, lest he put forth his hand, and take also of the tree of life, and eat and live forever: Therefore the Lord God sent him forth from the garden of Eden to till the ground from whence he was taken. So he drove out the man; and he placed at the east of the garden of Eden cherubims, and a flaming sword which turned every way, to keep the way of the tree of life."*

You will notice it said that God made coats of skin and clothed them. That is the first killing of animals, this is the first shedding of blood. The coats of skin were a covering for Adam and Eve.

Exodus 12:13 *"And the blood shall be to you for a token upon the houses where ye are: and when I see the blood, I will pass over you and the plague shall not be upon you to destroy you . . ."* The Lord sent an angel of death across the land of Egypt. He told His children to take the blood and place it upon the mantle, strike it on two sides of the posts of the door, for the children of God, no death would fall upon them, no plague would come upon them . . . the angel of death would see the blood and pass over. **There is life in the blood.**

All the sacrifices of man for sin were of no avail. The Lord God sent his only son, Jesus Christ . . . the perfect, pure unblemished, spotless Lamb of God for the sins of the world. Jesus went upon the cross at Calvary and freely gave his life that you and I could have eternal life. They nailed Jesus upon the cross that your sins and my sins would be washed away forever through His blood. **Life is in the blood.**

John 19:34, *"But one of the soldiers with a spear pierced his side, and forthwith came there out blood and water."* The blood of Jesus Christ, when it was shed upon Calvary, brought the only perfect gift and sacrifice for sin into the world. The blood of Jesus Christ washes away the sins of the world. There is life in the blood.

I John 1:7-9 *"But if we walk in the light, as he is in the light, we have fellowship one with another, and the blood of Jesus Christ his Son cleanseth us from all sin. If we say that we have no sin, we deceive ourselves and the truth is not in us. If we confess our sins, he is faithful and just to forgive us our sins, and to cleanse us from all unrighteousness."* When we come before God the Father, confessing our sins, asking Jesus to come into our heart and be our Lord and Saviour, then we have a right to the blood covering of Jesus Christ. We have the right to go to the Father and ask for forgiveness of our sins through the blood of Jesus.

Hebrews 10:19 *"Having therefore brethren boldness to enter into the holiest by the blood of Jesus."* We spiritually go into the very presence of God because we have the blood of Jesus Christ covering us. **Life is in the blood.**

Ephesians 1:7 *"In whom we have redemption through his blood, the forgiveness of sins, according to the riches of his grace."*

Revelations 12:11 *"And they overcame him by the blood of the Lamb and by the word of their testimony and they loved not their lives unto the death."*

Matthew 26:27-28 *". . . Drink ye all of it; for this is my blood of the New Testament, which is shed for many for the remission of sins."*

Jesus spoke those words at the Last Supper with his disciples. The believers today break bread and drink of the cup continually. Jesus said, *"As often as ye do this do it in remembrance of me."* The cup of the New Testament is symbolic of the blood of Jesus Christ, for through his blood, truly our sins have been remitted. **Life is in the blood.**

THE BATTLE RAGES ON

Ezekiel 16:6 *"And when I passed by thee, and saw thee polluted in thine own blood, I said unto thee when thou wast in thy blood, live; yea, I said unto thee when thou wast in thy blood, live."*

I knew that life-giving fluid was leaving me at a very rapid pace. There was no doubt in my mind that I was in trouble. I ran to the house, and as I got there, my wife, opened the back door and met me on the patio. I told them to get me some towels . . . get me a washcloth . . . get me anything they could grab. I had my arm tightly squeezed trying to stop the flow of blood. I couldn't. I wrapped a tourniquet above the elbow to cease the flow of this fluid that was taking my very life out of me. It only slowed it partially. I put another tourniquet just above the wound between the elbow and the wound and stopped it to a greater extent.

I still had not thought of anything except of the necessity to get to a hospital. I told my wife to grab all the towels she could muster together, that we had to get to the hospital, but to be calm, to not worry, everything was going to be all right. I had an unusual peace about me, an unusual calmness and clearness of mind.

As my wife drove us to the hospital, I sat there and I looked at my arm. I thought, "My Lord in heaven, what's happening! How could this happen to me! The Bible says that the angels are given charge over us, but yet here I sit. Was it because of my ignorance in handling the clippers? Was it something that I had done foolishly in a moment of not watching?" I didn't know. I knew one thing, that this was not from God. God is not the taker of life, He is the giver of life.

This was the work of the devil, but it would result in glory to God. I looked at my arm and I said, "Father this is not of you. Devil you are a liar and I bind you in the Name of Jesus! You'll not have victory! "

THE BATTLE RAGES ON

I had been tormenting the devil, setting people free through the power of the Holy Spirit. Now it was time to practice what I had been preaching to others.

It's one thing to minister to others and a totally different thing to live what you preach. Yet, when we serve God, we will either live what we preach or stop preaching. Why? The devil will single you out for attack. Attempt to kill you or at the least shut you down. How? Adversity!

Adversity had visited my home, it's either stand or fall. Practice what you preach or get out of town.

By now I knew there was no turning back. Jeremiah 33:3, *"Call unto me and I will answer thee and show thee great and mighty things which thou knowest not."*

Show me he did. After a wild ride to the emergency room. Two hours of surgery, I walked out of the hospital. My recovery was quick and sure. The battle had been hot and ferocious, yet I emerged victorious.

That day I learned an important lesson. Never let your guard down. *"Be sober, be vigilant; because your adversary the devil, as a roaring lion, walketh about, seeking whom he may devour."* I Peter 5:8

That day is forever frozen in my mind to remind me the battle rages on. Why? I had been ...

FIRST ON THE SCENE

Mike

Donnie

Natalie

56

Crank Up the Music, Let's Have Church

God is so good, who would have ever thought that God would call Tena and me to Pastor a church. Wow, now I realize, I have been enrolled in Holy Ghost University. As my dad used to say, "Son, it's on the job training."

All the institutions and books in the world cannot prepare you as life itself does.

It's not graduation day, it's just the beginning!

July 7, 1980, revival explodes, people come from everywhere. Salvations, healings, deliverances, and baptisms during every service, it's like a bomb has been dropped.

Moving in the spirit realm is the greatest of all experiences. Yet, you must **be careful** that you do not become comfortable with who you are and what God is doing through you.

CRANK UP THE MUSIC, LETS HAVE CHURCH.

A traveling singing group made up of people from all Christian walks of life arrive at the church. The man in charge tells me he has a lady in the group with problems, demons. Can you help? Yep! You have come to the right place and I am your man.

BE CAREFUL!

Service is over. Bring her into my office, a 10 X 10 carpeted walled office. Carpeted because the walls are paper thin. Small but okay. Tena and another lady join me.

"What is the problem lady?" "Voices begin to speak to me, my heart fills with rebellion," she said. "No problem, I'll pray for you."

BE CAREFUL!

I start to pray, she growls. Uh-oh! Excuse me, do I know you? Before I know what happens, she leaps to her feet reaches out at me and scratches my face. I grab her hands, forget the prayer, I am in trouble.

Chairs fly, plants move. Help! Somebody get me some help. Two big men (6' approximately 200 lbs.) that work with me in ministry, rush in. Grab her! Grab her! One grabs one arm the other grabs the other arm. Now, you devil, we have got you. Devil I command you... Bam! She kicks me. Oh you want some of me? I put a hammer lock on her head. Two women are pushed into a small corner praying. Three men are holding one medium size woman. One demon possessed woman bouncing us like rubber balls. Help!

"I told you to be careful, you have become too confident in yourself. Let her go," a voice said to me. I responded, "I bind you devil, if I let her go she will kill us all." Yet, the voice was of the Spirit, not of devils. My flesh was in the battle, God wanted to teach me something. "Let her go!" "Let her go?" "Let her go!" "Okay guys, let her go!" "What?" "Let her go!" "You have lost your mind Pastor she will kill us." "Let her go!"

Suddenly they let her go. God speaks, "Tell the devil to do what he is big enough to do." I obeyed and spoke as God said. She sat down and smiled.

My office is a wreck, three men are a wreck, and the two women are a wreck. Suddenly the power of God that I knew before comes upon me. The spirit speaks to my heart. *"... not by might, nor by power, but by my spirit, saith the Lord of hosts."* (Zechariah 4:6)

Devil I break your powers, come out in Jesus name! Gloriously saved and filled by the power of God. The moral? **Be careful of yourself when you're...**

FIRST ON THE SCENE

Here They Come

Wherever the spirit of revival is, it always pulls every nut, fruit, and flake walking around. People from everywhere with every kind of personality will come. It is great because God will manifest himself. That is what revival is all about, setting people free. It is not just church folks having more church, it is not just church folks ministering to church folks, it is a time of drawing the world to be delivered, healed, saved, and set free.

HERE THEY COME

The building is full to overflowing, revival is in the land. The Sunday morning message is coming forth with power. Suddenly a disturbance to my right. I keep on preaching. People begin to move their chairs. I keep on preaching. Then the unbelievable happens. A woman goes stiff as a board, the back of her neck and the heels of her feet are the only things touching the chair and the floor. What is this? Her feet begin to rise up off the floor, she is levitating. I am preaching. Without missing a beat, I move to where she is. Excuse me, do I know you? I put my hand in her mid section and push, then I place my foot in her middle and shove her to the floor. Devil! Come out! Church is on!

HERE THEY COME

Who is this little lady with the funny looking face? What was that? She is making some kind of weird noise during the service. "Brother – you sit behind her, if she starts that noise again just lay your hand gently on her shoulder." He did, she turned and slapped him. Oh brother, here we go again. Altar call, here she comes. One of the men said, "Don't worry

Pastor, I'll stand behind her in case of trouble." I am at the other end of this line, I glance toward the little woman and she makes her noise. My helper touches her on the shoulder, she turns and hits him in the stomach. I race toward her. What does this woman have on under her clothes, my God, it's a rubber suit! Excuse me, do I know you? You four foot devil from hell, loose her and let her go!

HERE THEY COME

"Pastor there's a lady out here who wants to bring her dog into the services." "What? Tie the dog to the fence outside." "But Pastor, she said her dog speaks in tongues." "Let him speak and do whatever else outside."

Thank God, a normal service. "What is this paper sack with tape?" "The lady with the dog left it for you." "Throw it in the car." We got home and opened the sack. What is this? Toe nail clippings from her dog. Oh Brother, just what I need. Sunday morning all is quite, a normal service, and a powerful message coming forth. What is that? A lady standing in the back. What is that in her hand? A stick with feathers hanging down shaking it up and down and mumbling something. Oh no, it is the lady with the tongue talking dog. Oh well, "Come out in Jesus name."

HERE THEY COME

Praise and Worship is always a vital part of revival, if not the very thing that sets the stage for a move of God. We have always had an "explosion of praise."

The church is packed, once again chairs are brought in. The people are standing, arms extended toward heaven. Who is that coming down the middle aisle, arms extended like an airplane, and head tilted back? Oh it is just another drunk coming to the Lord. As he makes his way toward the front, his hands slap the back of the heads of those on the left and right. I come down, spin him around, walk him back out to the entrance and cast the devil out. God sobered him up and saved him. If I had not shared this with the people, most would not have known what happened. They were lost in worship. You can be lost in God and still be **First on the scene**.

HERE THEY COME

Demon possessed, whacked out prophets and prophetesses, drunks, you name it, they will come. Is it an invasion from hell? No! I believe God sends them to a place that is not afraid to do what needs to be done. A place where there is a people willing to be...

FIRST ON THE SCENE

A Bus Load of What?

When revival explodes, the church services have no pattern. A normal (whatever that is) flow of Sunday a.m., p.m. and Wednesday services generally have a distinct pattern. Yet, when revival is flowing each is as powerful as the other.

Wednesday night service. Oh, brother, now who parked a school bus in front of the doors. Why didn't they park out away from the entrance?

The head usher meets me out in the parking lot with a strange look on his face as he proclaims, "Pastor, there's a whole bus load of weird people here, they ran out of gas and want help."

A BUS LOAD OF WHAT?

Just what I need, not one weirdo at a time, but a whole bus load. "What do you mean weird?" I replied. "Pastor they all have on long white robes, their heads are shaved and some have pony-tails coming out in different parts of their heads. Some in back, on top, the side and they all live in the bus. I think there are about eight or ten of them."

As I walk to the front door of the building, I notice the bus is painted white. As I step into the building, there they are all sitting on the back row. As I step in the usher tells them I am the Pastor. They all stand and begin to bow with hands folded under their chin in an oriental style.

Now that's more like it. It's about time that the devil starts to bow. "Who are you?" I ask. "Children of god," they proclaim. "Yea, sure, but what god?" I say to myself.

What a sad sight, people searching for truth, yet so deceived. They ask for help, my first thought is "no way, I'll not help a bunch of weirdos." Yet deep inside I know God had directed their path. God was up to something and I was not about to get in the way.

"You'll have to sit in our service, I'll talk to you after church. If you leave the building I will not help you." That did it, they are desperate. No gas, no food, no god. They will stay.

The music explodes, our people are rejoicing. The white robed weirdos stare in amazement. The Word that I had prepared goes to the sidelines. God has different plans.

The Holy Spirit takes control, the Word comes forth in power, the truth is exploding. Never had these people seen true worship, nor had they ever heard the truth. I preach on "This one called Jesus." I remember using Acts 17 where Paul encountered a whole city of weirdos. The people of Athens had erected altars to every god they could think of. Paul observed their zeal, found an altar erected to the "unknown god." He said, "It's him that I come to declare to you." I now find myself declaring the one true God to a deceived people. Truth comes forth – line upon line, precept upon precept.

"Now!" I hear the Spirit proclaim within me. I call forth all those who want Jesus to save them, fill them and free them. Without hesitation the whole bunch of white robed weirdos step into the aisle, as they walk forward God touches them, tears fill their eyes, joy fills their hearts as the truth sets them free. Salvation descends!

We filled their bus with gas, gave them food and some traveling money, prayed over them and told them to go home to their friends and family and tell what great things God had done for them.

Wow! Is God awesome or what? Now we are plundering hell and populating heaven by the bus load. Why...

FIRST ON THE SCENE

Party Crasher

Whenever you obey God at all cost, you will not only see the miraculous, but you will be used in a way you could not ever imagine.

Church is over. A woman in our church brings up a lady to meet us. "Pastor this is____, she came tonight because she is tormented. Years ago she sacrificed her baby to Satan and has dedicated her life to him."

"Woman do you want to be free?" "I can't, it is too late." "If it were not too late, would you want to be free." "Yes!"

It is never too late! This is the hour of deliverance! Satan I bind you! Watch out, you have been here before. She tries to scratch my face. I grab her hands and with all the power of God available, I shouted "come out!" She falls limp. We raise her up to her feet, she is saved and filled with the Spirit.

PARTY CRASHER

She begins to share how she agreed with the devil to come to our church and disrupt our services. She said, "I stood in your parking lot and prayed with Satan to destroy your services." Satan told her, "We will crash this party and destroy this church." I said, "What happened?" She made a statement you had better never forget. "He ran out on me and would not come in." Why? "Greater is He that is in us than he that is in the world. Behold I give you power over all the power of the devil?" That is why you should always be...

FIRST ON THE SCENE!

WOW!
We're Pastors

No, I am not making
shadow pictures of our
dog on the wall. I am
preaching, pay attention.

He will set your feet to dancing.

Crank up the music. Tena
on piano - Mike on drums.

African Devils

As we each travel through life, it seems as though we forget, *"The steps of a good* (righteous through the blood) *man* (mankind) *are ordered* (established) *by the Lord: and he delighteth in his way."* (emphasis mine) Psalms 37:23

God ordains our steps, yet sometimes we are convinced that because of what is happening to us and around us, that surely this must be a devil. Often those things that bring discomfort and challenges to our plans and purposes are positioned by God to bring us to an awareness of where we truly are in our walk with Him. Usually one of two things is revealed. 1) We are not as strong as we thought, or 2) We realize how big God has become inside of us since the last time we were tested by life. Either way, we grow.

Have you ever been caught in turmoils of life, convinced beyond a doubt, the devil was managing your struggles? Right in the middle of your discomfort and challenges shout, "Devil I bind you!" only to hear the voice of the Spirit respond back, "Excuse me, I am not a devil, and besides that you can't bind me." Boy, how embarrassed I've been when I've been in that position. I sure am glad no one was there to hear me.

Each encounter of life will be used by God to develop you for His purposes for you. I am sure of one thing, that which God pursues will be overtaken and His purpose will be accomplished. (Acts 9)

WOW! Am I growing or what? Years of development, encounter after encounter, developing and strengthening me. Pastoring an explosive church. Three years of revival resulting in hundreds being saved, baptized in the Spirit, healed and delivered. A church of 150 growing to over 2000. A campus of 1.2 acres to a campus of 10 acres. The awesomeness of God. One thing I know for sure *"... not by might, nor by Power, but by my Spirit, saith the Lord of hosts."* Zech. 4:6. This work is a sovereign work of God. All I am doing is holding on for the wildest ride of my life.

AFRICA

I have dreamed of Africa all my life. Believing one day to go on a great safari. I guess as a kid I saw too many Tarzan movies. But God! I am here! Nigeria West Africa. WOW! My mental pictures just blew apart. No Tarzan! No monkey! No elephant! No zebra! Just a land full of millions of people hungry for God. A hunger and power far beyond what I have ever known. Warfare? Power over the devil? Prayer? Faith? That's the middle name of these people. Never have I found such power among a people on the earth. I suppose it comes from a daily battle of years of oppression. Oppressed by man. Having to believe God for everything. Food, shelter, clothing, work, everything and anything that we take for granted must be fought for in Nigeria. The results? A people of God with great power and faith.

YOU ARE WELCOME!

Criss-crossing the nation of Nigeria. Preaching in two churches a day, morning and night. Some places two to three hundred, other places four to five thousand, some ten to fifteen thousand. Outdoor crusade in Lagos over thirty thousand in attendance. My God, how you love me, to allow me to be involved in such a move of your Spirit. I am being changed into a different man. When Saul was anointed by Samuel, the Prophet, the Word says, "*And the Spirit of the Lord will come upon thee, and thou shalt prophesy with them, and shalt be turned into another man.*" I Samuel 10:6. The anointing comes by impartation and association! You cannot travel for 21 days, preaching under the anointing day after day and not be consumed. No phones ringing, no T.V., no friends to talk to, no one asking questions, no appointments, no outside world. Pray, study, preach. WOW, have I died and gone to heaven or what?

Everywhere I go in Nigeria, I hear the same thing. "You are welcome!" A people so full of joy and gladness that someone would travel so far and drive so long to bring them the "Good News." Yet, I hear a dark whisper, "You are not welcome – this is my land and my people." Is that right! Well, time will tell devil!

Lagos, Nigeria, twenty to thirty thousand people fill the grounds. "Tonight you will preach," said my host. I have been preaching for two days at their church conference. Thousand in attendance at the church, yet what I was now looking at, I was not prepared for. A sea of people. Forget reading from your Bible, most of these people don't have one. The Spirit explodes within me. WOW, I am preaching Jesus from Genesis to Revelation, everything I have ever learned is flowing out of me.

BAM! The grounds are dark, no lights, a power failure again. I stop, I wait, people are quiet watching me, waiting on my response. Let's see, in America what would I do? No good, this is Africa. One minute seems like an hour. A voice spoke inside me. Close the meeting, the lights always stay out for hours. I pause, I wait, 5 minutes no lights. There it is again, an explosion inside me, the Holy Spirit. I shout at the top of my lungs. "Devil, we will not be defeated, get your hands off the lights. I command you in Jesus name, stop your interferences." Nothing! Sweat pouring over my body, nerves or heat? I can hear my own heart beating, my ears are ringing, my mind said "why did you open your big mouth? You should have left this alone." Explosion! Once again the Spirit pours through me. "Devil, did you hear me? Leave!" Suddenly – lights! The crowd explodes. I cried out – "Jesus is Lord, Jesus has power over the devil, you must come to Jesus, Now!" Suddenly, the crowd surges forward, over 2500 people saved in one sweep of God's power.

The host is closing the service, he says to me "Pray." Pray? OK! I start out with my U.S. style prayer, then, yep, you guessed it, "Explosion within!" Power of prayer like I have never known. Then just as suddenly, we begin to praise God for the souls that were saved and thanking Him for healing and changing our lives, I can't hear myself anymore, thirty thousand people with one voice, it sounds like the rush of Niagra Falls.

I step back, God speaks, "Watch the child on your far left." A two to three year old child, his mother picking him up trying to get him to stand. No good, his legs are like rubber. Praise beyond my wildest imagination continues. I turn to my wife and tell her, "Watch that little boy, God is going to do something." Ten to fifteen minutes of solid praise. Suddenly the child stands! The mother begins to leap up and down, others around her join in. Then the boy starts to run, like a wave the news spreads over the crowd. They surge forward. My God, a crippled child healed only to be crushed by the crowd. A man leaps from the platform, swoops the child up and stands him beside me on the platform. They ask the mother about the child. Born deaf, blind and crippled. Now running and leaping and praising God.

LOOK OUT DEVIL HERE I COME!

Agbor, a village in the Benin City area, we've shipped a large 3000-seat tent over to set up for crusades and birthing churches. The tent is full, thousands are on the outside. I have the privilege of preaching again.

I am closing my message. I begin to lead the people in a favorite statement of theirs. "Up-Up Jesus" I would cry – "Down-Down satan" they would reply. Power builds. People are running forward to get saved and healed. Wild is not sufficient to describe this place. Suddenly someone pushes a child into my hands. Six to seven years old. Boy or girl? I can't tell. Must be a girl, long plaited pigtails cover the head. There is so much noise, I can't hear anything. What do I pray for? Well, when in doubt – cast it out! I am praying to break the powers of darkness off this child's life. I have no idea what the need is. Watch out! What's this! The Pastor rushes toward me from the side. What's in his hand? A knife? No! It's scissors! Scissors? Before I knew what happened, he held the child's head, snip, snip, pigtails are falling to the ground. Boy, are you in trouble or what? This kid's mother is going to be furious. The last pigtail hits the dirt, I am watching in amazement. Suddenly the crowd explodes, dancing and shouting – "Up-Up Jesus, Down-Down satan." Me? I don't have a clue!

When we finally settled down, the Pastor explained. As a baby the child was dedicated to satan. The covenant between satan and the parents is symbolized by never cutting the hair. They believe if the hair is cut, the person will die instantly. WOW! With every pigtail that hit the ground, a cry would go up. Devil you're a liar!

Enugu, Nigeria, a large city in the east. Three thousand people cram the building. Seven days of services. Six hundred in one service saved.

The next night it seems the same six hundred were filled with the Holy Spirit. The gifts are flowing in power. I am teaching a day session, approximately four hundred Pastors are present. Right in the middle of my message, God decides to do His thing. A prophecy pours from my lips, "As in the days of Ananias and Sapphira so shall it be today. If those who represent me to my people do not purge sin from their life." Once again I was not prepared for what was about to happen. Suddenly a man was lifted up and flung backward, flying through the air and landing two to three rows back. Screaming out, "God please don't kill me – please don't kill me." Rolling in the dirt toward the platform crying the whole time. Then falling out like a dead man. Suddenly the altar fills, leaders of churches crying out to God in repentance. God shaking His church.

THE LONGEST DAY

Each service in Africa lasts no less than four to five hours. Yet, once again, I would be a part of the extraordinary.

Closing the conference in Enugu on Easter Sunday. The service started at 8:30 am and concluded at 6:30 am the next day. My God, 22 hours! Every church represented (76) had their choir sing. Bible school students graduated. Offerings were received. The Word was preached. You name it, we did it.

Midnight, the power of praise has taken over, the building is trembling under the power of praise. Suddenly a roar goes up in the balcony. What's happening? I don't know! I just know this, the Holy Ghost has taken over. What are these men carrying on their shoulder? WOW, another burst of energy in another location. What's going on? People begin to scram. Fire! Fire! Fire! I look for the nearest exit, "Feet don't fail me now." Wait a minute! This is a block building with a tin roof. It can't burn. It was not an alarm of a fire in the building, it was a call for the Fires of God to fall.

Suddenly men began to drop their cargo. Women! Women? Their legs tied at the ankles, hitting the floor one – two – three – on and on it went. From all over the building, they were bringing them. I look down in front of me as they unload a woman at my feet. "Excuse me – do I know you?" No, the Almeda devil could never exist over here. WOW! Her face is pointed, her tongue darts in and out, she's slithering about like a snake. I don't think I know how to handle this.

Then before I knew what was happening, women with quart and gallon jars of oil rush in pouring oil over them, the crowd crying out "Fire – Fire – Fire." Men fall down beside these women, laying hands and commanding "Come out!" Look out devil, here I come! One giant leap I am on the floor, oil flying everywhere, sweating like a pig at a barbeque. Boy, if my church could see me now. When the dust settled, over 60 women, lay quietly on the floor, weeping before God. They told me later this was a common thing in some areas. Women go under water in the streams and rivers taking on the spirit of the water, then going to church meetings to disrupt and put fear in the people. Sorry devil, "Greater is He that is in me, than he that is in the world."

Ilesa, Nigeria, "Brother Ford we want to show you our revival centers." "Great, let's go!" Revival center? This looks more like a bunch of storage buildings. As we walked from building to building, I could not believe what I was seeing and hearing. People with hopelessness were brought here, given up on by everybody. Brought here to be healed and delivered or die. No turning back. Row after row of dirt floor, tin buildings. One for those with lung problems, they looked like walking skeletons. One for those with skin diseases, flesh rotting away. One for lunatics. WOW! Chained to posts like some horror movie.

A large building in the center, "We bring them here for prayer" our hosts said. Twenty-four hours a day prayer is made for these people. While some eat or sleep, others are praying and crying out for those in need. They bring a girl before me, "She has demons, she can't sleep, she's full of fear, she's..." Before they could finish the Holy Spirit explodes again. My hands grip both sides of her head. "Come out!" I shouted as we both fell to the ground. I get up, look down at her, she jerks and grows limp. We stand her up. She smiles for the first time in two years and proclaims "I am free." Wow, the awesomeness of God.

DEVIL IN A JAR

Would you like to see a devil Brother Ford? We have one in a jar! What? A devil in a jar! This I must see. In a moment a man returns with a fruit jar. A white slim liquid is in it, in the middle is a hairy looking object. Excuse me devil, did you get trapped or what? I could not believe my eyes. Somebody explain to me how something supernatural turned into the natural.

In Africa one of the forms of devil worship is called "Ju-Ju." A person takes an object and calls upon it to empower them. In this case a "button with string wrapped around it." A lady made the object, prayed and chanted then swallowed it. They said, the people never pass the object, somehow it remains inside of them until they encounter a child of God and a power greater, then out it comes.

This is too much! One thing I have discovered. Each country has it's own unique devils. I know there is only one devil but many demons. Demons manifest among people according to their beliefs and cultures. Yet, I know something else. No matter where or what, when a child of God commands "Come out!" Out they come, the devil has no choice. He is defeated!

Lagos, Nigeria, a world conference is being held. Pastors and Leaders from all over Nigeria and the world gather with ten to fifteen thousand people. Day after day, night after night the anointing builds. It's the last night the host Pastor is under an anointing stronger than I have ever seen. He calls all Pastors to come forward, the power of God explodes as he anoints us with oil, an impartation is taking place. We'll never be the same again. "We're going to lay hands on everybody in the building," he proclaims. What? You've got to be kidding. How do you lay hands on fifteen thousand people? He positions each of us in front of sections of people. I am standing there looking into the faces of 800 to a thousand people. My mind is half U.S., half Nigeria. Who's this beside me. Two men on either side, one has a bucket, looks like a mop bucket, maybe I should get a mop. I don't know. What's in the bucket? Oil! My God, two gallons of oil. Suddenly, my host is praying, people are shouting so loud you can't hear yourself think. I am trying to figure out what and how I am supposed to accomplish the impossible. Corporate prayer continues, power is building, I am still thinking (U.S. brain). Suddenly a power from on high hits me, the host shouts, NOW! An explosion! Before I know what's happening, I am dipping my hands in the oil bucket. Not a U.S. two finger dip, I am talking about an elbow dip. Just as suddenly, I leap upon the first bench, arms spread out like an airplane, running from bench to bench, hitting people with my hands, arms and body. Front to back, back to front, side to side, I run. People falling out, some remain standing, some lifting their hands in praise, others crying out to God. Demons crying out. WOW! I feel like David. "I can run through a troop and leap over a wall." Suddenly it's over! It looks like a bomb has been dropped. I am astonished! Not a dry thread on me, oil from the top of my head to the soul of my feet, trembling under the power of God. Without a doubt, I will never be the same again.

My journey is over in Africa, yet it has only begun for my life. As I return, I am consumed by the anointing of God. Once you've tasted God's awesomeness there is no turning back. Now that I have seen God's power displayed in a way I had never known, I realize I am a threat to the devil's kingdom more now than ever before. I've tasted combat in a new way. WOW! I thought the devil hated me before, but now he is raging mad. Determined to destroy me, my family and ministry.

Poor devil, he's so frustrated, try as he may, he can't do it. "*For the eyes of the Lord run to and fro throughout the whole earth, to show himself strong in the behalf of them whose heart is perfect toward him...*" II. Chron. 16:9 Here devil, devil, devil. Come out wherever you are. Here devil, devil devil. I am looking for you. Why? I want to be...

FIRST ON THE SCENE

Lagos Stadium - Approx. 30 thousand in attendance

Preaching at Lagos Stadium

Tent meeting at Agbor

Women possessed - acting like snakes.

Lunatic chained to post.

Witchcraft items "Ju-Ju"

Divine impartation into Pastors lives.

Divine impartation into my life.

Left side of platform of the meeting in which we anointed everyone with oil. Awesome!

Swami Who?

With the power and anointing of God in my life to "plunder hell and populate heaven," I've become a real threat to the devil. My life and ministry is charging hell with a squirt gun!

Often when I preach especially when I travel to Africa, I ask the people a question that always shakes them, "How many of you have your name written down in Hell?"

The response is always the same. Silence, as the look on their face seems to say, "He did mean heaven, didn't he? I don't want my name in hell's book, I've got enough problems!!!"

Acts 19 reveals a powerful truth. When the seven sons of Sceva tried to cast out devils like Paul, the demons responded, *"Jesus I know, Paul I know, but who are you?"*

Jesus, Paul and the disciples were known in hell. Why? "Plundering hell and populating heaven!" My ministry thrust became very evident from the beginning. "Torment the devil!" And torment him I have.

My secretary buzzes my office, "Pastor, there are two gentlemen out here who want to see you if you have a moment." "Who are they," I replied. "They say they're from the Hindu temple." Oh brother, just what I need, idol worshippers. Then that still small voice said, "Go, I want to teach you something."

Every location that our church has occupied has pulled heathen worshippers. In our old location, the Jehovah witnesses built their hall across the street. Now the Hindus built a temple down the street. I might as well accept the fact that my ministry is like that of Mt. Carmel when Elijah proclaimed ..."*The God that answereth by fire, let him be God...*"

Brother John Osteen always reminded me that the lost, whether they be our neighbors or the tribes of people in the dark regions of the world, must hear the "Good News."

I adjusted my attitude and walked out into the reception area. "Swami _____ would like to meet you." They said as they bowed before me. This sect of people worship over two million gods, having twelve main gods as their focus of worship, to them I am a "holy man," respected for my ministry.

I step outside. WOW! A $150,000.00 Rolls Royce awaits me for a two block ride. More men bowing to me. The car pulls up to their front door. Hundreds are there to worship their demons. I step out, all begin to bow. I think to myself, "Get on with your bad self, Richard." They told me to remove my shoes, no problem – I like to be barefooted anyway.

A door opens to my left, people fall to their knees and bow, it's the Swami himself. Reminds me of the story in Judges 3 where Ehud had a dagger hidden under his clothes as he had a private audience with King Eglon of Moab, who was oppressing the people. The Bible said he was a fat man. Fat devils, skinny devils, makes no difference. I have the sword of the Spirit to cut him down.

Suddenly someone is trying to force me to my knees to bow. No way! Stiff as a board I turn and say, "I bow to no one but Jesus."

They lead me behind the Swami. Boy is this place bare, no furniture. Oh, I see, women on the right, men on the left, everyone bows on the floor before the idols.

Twelve grotesque statues face the people. Human bodies, animal heads, they bow up and down as they chant. What's that outside? Looks like a bunch of barbeque pits built on the ground. Yep, it is. The place where they prepare the food for the demons, they call for them to fellowship with them. I didn't know the devil liked barbeque.

Into the room with the Swami. There he is sitting up on a huge pillow. Maybe he's got trouble with his bottom. The interpreter tells me that the Swami is glad I am there and that we are both working for the same purposes. Give me a break! He shares his life's journey with me, how he has been reincarnated over and over until he has reached his godhead.

Then they ask if I wanted to say anything. Yes! But first I want my picture taken with this devil. No one is going to believe this. Fun is over, time to preach.

For the next thirty minutes, I proclaimed Jesus as the only true Lord and Saviour and Jehovah as the one and only true God.

I wish I could tell you that the Swami and all the people converted to Christ, but I cannot. The Swami just sat there listening with this stare on his face. I don't know what God did in their lives, but I do know what He did for me. He reminded me that these people represent millions around the world who are blinded and must be set free. Oh, another thing, I discovered my name is written in hell. Why?...

FIRST ON THE SCENE

Excuse me! Do I know you?

Who Wants to See Me?

"A man's gifts maketh room for him, and bringeth him before great men" Proverbs 18:16. It's amazing what God has prepared for those who love Him and serve Him. Having answered His call to abandon all and follow Him has resulted in a journey I would have never been able to comprehend.

Standing beside, serving and ministering with God's generals has been an amazing part of my life. Who am I that God would position me for these encounters? Each encounter is like a Joshua with Moses, Elisha with Elijah, as God's elite impart into my life.

WHO WANTS TO SEE ME?

My phone at home rings, the voice on the other end says, "Richard, this is John Osteen, I would like to meet with you in my office." WOW! Brother Osteen has called me many times to encourage Tena and me, but never has he called for a private meeting. My father in the Lord, the man God positioned in my life in the very beginning of my ministry, the man whom I have studied, the "General" that has impacted my life more than anyone else, wants to see me.

As I arrived that day it was the most exciting day of my life, what an honor. Myself and four or five other Pastors were there. Brother Osteen was approaching 50 years of ministry and asked us to help make it a memorable event.

"Tena, Tena, you're not going to believe this, Brother Osteen wants me to teach a workshop during his conference to celebrate his 50 years of ministry." Together we cried and rejoiced knowing that God had opened a great and effectual door. We had always supported everything Brother Osteen and Dodie had ever done, now it's harvest time.

That week has been revealed as a point in time in my life in which God elevated my life and ministry to a new level. My involvement with my father in the Lord opened vast doors around the nations of the world, developing relationships with ministers that would not have otherwise had happened. I had the privilege of overseeing and producing many of Brother Osteen's books in Nigeria as well as his TV ministry in Lagos. Each time I think of Brother Osteen, a cry within rises up, "My Father, My Father." Why? Because of the anointing! The anointing is transferred by impartation and association. I was privileged to receive both.

WHO WANTS TO SEE ME?

Every encounter is a special encounter. Serving God is an adventure in faith. Experiencing the awesomeness of God is the ultimate experience. The privilege of knowing, supporting and ministering with God's Generals is beyond description.

Dr. Lester Sumrall laying hands on me imparting years of anointing and wisdom into my life. Listening to his stories as we fellowship over lunch together of how God used him all over the world to "Tear the devil's kingdom down."

Traveling to the foreign fields, Mexico, Guatemala, Venezuela, Israel, Jordan, Egypt, Africa and Europe has placed a new hunger for God within me as I have seen the faces and hear the cry of people crying out for help.

YOU WANT TO SEE WHO?

T.L. and Daisy Osborn! Everywhere I travel, especially Africa, this man and woman have preceded me. They have impacted the world in a dramatic way. Now, here is Tena and I sitting in their office in Tulsa, OK. listening to and being instructed and encouraged by two of God's great generals. Is God good or what? A relationship that would continue into the future as they would come to our church to minister. Sending us everything they had ever written. Laying hands on us and proclaiming "Do great things for God!" Daisy proclaiming to Tena, "Tena you are a daughter of destiny."

WHO WANTS TO SEE ME?

Traveling and ministering with Dr. Buddy Harrison in Nigeria; exploding with the anointing as he laid hands on myself, my son and son-in-law. Working together with him and Pat (daughter and son-in-law of Kenneth Hagin) in the great ministry God entrusted them with, "F.C.F. Int." A man and ministry used to mold and shape my ministry to produce quality leadership skills in my life and the life of those whom God has sent to assist us.

WHO WANTS TO SEE US?

The King of Benin! Buddy and I had been ministering at a great conference and churches as we travel across Nigeria. Now the King of Benin wants to see us.

We arrive at a large building with chairs on the left and right of a great platform with large space between the two sides of the chairs. We were told to bring a gift. I brought several copies of my book "Prayer – The Key to Power" to present to the King. Being a King he understood power, but he did not know Jesus and this book would present Jesus to him.

Trumpet sounds – young men in clothing like the movie "The King & I." Each carrying a huge sabre, escorting the King. The King enters preceded by women casting flower petals and serving the King. "Go on with your bad self, King."

After all the formalities, it's our turn to address the King. "King," I say, "Today is a day of honor for me, and honor to stand before so powerful a ruler. I bring you a gift on behalf of one more powerful than you. Jesus – the King of Kings." Suddenly there's a stirring among the people. Did I say something wrong? Then I presented him the books. He looks strangely at them and then replies, "I cannot allow this book into my kingdom. I am power." Oh, now I understood, he feels threatened. So for the next five to ten minutes, I shared the "Good News" of Jesus. He settles, smiles and says, "I will read this great book and share it with my leaders." Glory! We just invaded another kingdom.

WHO WANTS TO SEE ME?

R.W. Schambach is coming to town with his tent and needs as many Pastors to help as possible. WOW! What a privilege, I like his style.

Meeting is over, Pastors more established than I, have been appointed to take certain responsibilities. No problem, I am just glad to be a part.

My phone rings, "Hello Brother Ford, this is _____, I am not going to be able to handle the ushers for Brother Schambach, I talked with his office and they OK'd you, if you can help." Yes!

Once again, God has opened a great door.

Revival! Night after night, personally helping R.W. Schambach, standing next to him as his personal assistant, watching him move under the power of God. WOW! Does it get any better than this.

The last night, hundreds have been saved, filled and healed.

What a week! Uh-oh, I've heard this before. We're going to lay hands on everybody under the tent. Across the platform ramp they come. Bill and Renee Morris has the organ and music pumping. People piled up before the altar. Some out under the power, others dancing. Is this Pentecost or what?

Suddenly, Brother Schambach walks over to me, "Take the service, close it when you're through, I am out of here." What?

How do you take over a Pentecostal riot? People are rushing to me for prayer, I am laying hands on everybody, I have no idea what they need. The noise is overwhelming as they shout and dance. Reminds me of Africa.

A woman pushes through, shoves her son in front of me, ten to eleven years old. She says something; I can't understand her. Oh well, when in doubt, cast it out. I lay both hands on the side of his head over his ears, shout "Come out!"

Suddenly he jumps, looks at his mother, they say something, they run and shout, those who know them run and shout. Now wait a minute! Somebody tell me what's happening? Born deaf and now can hear! Look out my turn to run, jump and shout.

God is so good. Ten years later I am leaving my office. As I walk to my car a man approaches me. "Hi, Pastor Ford, do you remember me?" he said with a broken speech. "No, I don't, refresh my memory." "I am the boy under the tent, you laid hands on me, now I can hear. " We hugged, we laughed. Is God good or what?

WHO WANTS TO SEE ME?

The honor of knowing Jesse and Cathy Duplantis from 1981 to this present time. The hours and days of fellowship together in our home as they not only help develop our ministry but impart the anointing and wisdom of God to us personally. Speaking into our lives has forever changed us.

"Hey Richard, this is Jesse, Cathy and I want you and Tena to come to our home in New Orleans." "Wow, Jesse, that would be great, but we are loaded down with ministry right now," I replied. "Forget it, that's why you need to come, besides I've already bought you tickets, get on the plane!"

Ministry is fun and ministry is great, yet there is a stress and pressure that will consume you if you're not careful. Right now, "Stress" is my middle name. God knows what I need, "A couple of days with a nut" should change my perspective.

If there was ever a "nut," it's Jesse Duplantis. People often ask me, "Is Jesse really as crazy as some of his stories imply?" You don't know the half of it. He's consumed with a spirit of lunacy. This guy will cause you to collapse in laughter; yet the anointing God has placed on his life will explode in revelation and set you free.

Tena, throw some clothes in a bag we're going to see Jesse and Cathy. Now? Now! Take your car and leave it at the church so when we get back I don't have to go home, I've a thousand things to do when we get back. "Stress"

As usual, we seem to be running on a tight schedule, no time for delays.

I pull up behind our church building and wait. Where is that woman, don't she know we're on a schedule? "Stress" Five minutes pass, Oh brother, we're in trouble, where is that woman? Sitting in her car in front of the church! "Stress"

Have you lost your mind woman. I told you to park behind the church. (I think) No you didn't! Yes I did! No you didn't! "Stress" Shut up and get your car to the back of the church.

I start my motor, open the passenger door, no time to waste, we're late. "Stress" Tena pulls to the back. Look at that woman, she thinks we have all day. Run woman! Get in the car!

She steps into the car, I am not waiting for the door to close, she can close it while I drive. Vavooomm! I shoot out of the parking lot. Bump! Stop, she shouts. What was that, what did I run over? My shoe! Your shoe? How did you drop your shoe? It's supposed to be on your foot! My God woman, get the shoe, we're late! "Stress"

Forty minute drive to the airport, no talking, just heavy breathing and sweat. "Stress" Park the car, jump on the shuttle. Go to the gate. What? Wrong gate! Don't tell Tena I fouled up, let her think it's her fault.

Come on woman, get ahead of me, walk fast or we're going to miss our plane. "Stress" What's wrong with this woman? She's walking like one leg is three inches shorter than the other. Slip through the gate, fall into our seat. Hot, sweaty, mad and stressed. For one and one half hours the mad man from Gadara has been in control. Now? "Sweety's back!" "Honey, is something wrong with your leg?" I ask, in my perfected "sweety voice." No! She shot back. Then honey, why are you limping? You ran over my shoe and broke the heel! Holding up her shoe, the heel missing and the rest pushed out of shape. We looked at each other and exploded in laughter.

"Tena, what's wrong with your leg?" Jesse asks as we arrive.

Richard ran over my shoe! Oh brother, this is all Jesse needs. "What's wrong with you boy, don't you know how to drive?" Leave it alone Jesse! We all laugh, but Jesse won't leave it alone. "Come on! We'll get you another pair of shoes," said Jesse as his teeth shine like a new dime.

I thought, good he's going to bless my wife. Think again! Shoes need a new purse, new purse and shoes need a new belt.That will be $215.00 please. "Pay the woman, Richard, you're the one that destroyed the shoe," said Jesse. Oh brother Jesse strikes again. Oh well, I talked him out of two pillows on the bed that we slept on. We're not even, but I'm better off.

WHO WANTS TO SEE ME?

I begin to open my mail. Oral Roberts University, I wonder what this is?

"Dear Pastor Ford, Dr. Oral Roberts request your presence at a special meeting to be held on the 62nd floor of the City of Faith hospital building." Who me? Must be a mistake. My secretary calls and confirms the invitation. WOW! It's true, it's for me!

With great excitement, Tena and I arrive in Tulsa, OK. As we stepped off the elevator, we stepped into the "Who's Who" of the church world. Anybody and everybody that was somebody was there. We felt out of place but honored. We walked about, people introducing themselves, "Hello, I am Richard Ford and this is my wife Tena." Strange looks on their faces as if to say "Richard who?" No matter, God's plan, I am here.

Tena and I are not pushy, however we always sit as close to the front as possible wherever we go. It seems there are always seats open up front. We settle in. Brother Roberts opens the meeting, leading us in prayer then shares his heart with us. WOW! Me at a private meeting with "God's Generals."

Brother Roberts completed his meeting then said "Find someone, grab their hand and pray for one another." What was about to happen, I was not prepared for. Brother Roberts turned to me. Took my hand and said pray for me. WOW! Angels are singing, smoke fills the room. I am touching Oral Roberts! I am about to pray personally for Oral Roberts. "Too much!" What did I pray? I don't have a clue, I am on a cloud.

Then he looks at me and said, "What can I pray for you about?" Oh no, my brain is numb. I think I just went brain dead.

Watch this! You think God doesn't have a sense of humor?

What can Oral Roberts pray for me? Oh my God, a modern Apostle of faith, a man used by God in a miracle ministry that has been surpassed by none. The man that has defied the kingdom of darkness. Building a great university and city of faith, wants to pray for me.

Watch this, ignorance gone to seed. I had been working on my house a few weeks before and something had bit me on the forehead. I suspect it might have been a spider. A small round open sore had developed like a spider bite, it was healing very slowly.

What can I pray for you for? Anointing? Financial blessing? Miracle ministry? Ministry growth? Oh No! Not for Mr. Brain dead. I leaned toward Brother Roberts, pointed to the sore and said, "I think a spider bit me, will you lay hands on it and pray," I said as I closed my eyes in great anticipation and expectation.

Brother Roberts voice spoke forth, "I am not touching that nasty thing" and brushed his hand on top of my head. The music stopped, angels ceased singing, the cloud lifted. I sat there like a bump on a log. I wanted to choke myself. What an idiot!

Brother Roberts hugged me, prayed for me and asked God to bless me and walked off into the sunset.

When I realized what I had done, I broke out in laughter and joy like I had never experienced before. I may be nuts but God is still on the throne and one short hug and prayer would forever change my life.

Join Me!

The doorbell rings, it's my friend and covenant partner, Tommy Burchfield.

God had brought Tena and me into covenant relationship with Tommy and Rachel many years before. The joy that comes in being a part of developing the largest and most powerful Full Gospel Camp in the U.S. is indescribable.

There are no accidents with God. Every encounter has a purpose. Tommy had traveled with me to Nigeria where we ministered to multitudes.

It was during this time I had the opportunity to see first hand the depth of God's calling on Tommy's life as thousands of young people were drawn to him and the anointing God had deposited in him.

During this time, not only would our covenant together grow stronger, but something far deeper was being birthed. Texas Bible Institute!

Upon Tommy's return, he revealed God had spoken to him to begin T.B.I., WOW – God is awesome! Not only the largest camp, but a Bible School which is rapidly becoming the only one of it's kind in the U.S. directed toward the ages of 17-25. Raising up an army for God.

Now he asks, will you and Tena join Rachel and me and serve on the Board of Regents of T.B.I.? Yes! Together we will torment the devil.

Devil you've got a problem. Why? Thousands being developed to be...

FIRST ON THE SCENE

JOIN ME!

Jerry Savelle sitting in my office waiting for the service to start, looked at me and said "Richard, I would love for you and Tena to join Carolyn and me for our celebration of 30 years in ministry."

Once again I knew God's favor was at work in my life. Not because of the invitation, for many have been invited.

I heard the call of the Holy Spirit deep within, I knew something more lay ahead.

Four days of glory as we joined hundreds from around the world for the great celebration.

The last day exposed the deep pull of the Holy Spirit as Jerry and Carolyn shared their hearts openly concerning the call of God on their lives. Then it happened; **join me**!

An open door to step into a deeper covenant relationship by serving on the Presidents Cabinet. A group of people chosen by Jerry and Carolyn with like vision and purpose to help impact the world.

Tena and I responded with great excitement – yes, we join with you in a deeper covenant relationship.

Together we will be...

FIRST ON THE SCENE

JOIN ME!

My secretary informs me that there is a call from Greg Mauro with Morris Cerullo Ministries. Uh-oh, here we go again.

"Pastor Ford, Dr. Morris Cerullo wanted me to call and ask if you would be open to hosting the South Texas "Fresh Fire Believers' Breakthrough Rally."

Once more, 'the wonders of God.' Who am I that God, would do such a thing for? It's His favor!

Having never met Dr. Cerullo I eagerly awaited his arrival. Knowing that the anointing comes by impartation and association and I was about to be exposed to both.

An explosion of God's awesome power and anointing hit the church. One night that would forever change our church and my life.

As we arrived back at the airport, Dr. Cerullo layed his hands upon me, asking God to pour out a fresh call and anointing upon my life. Once again impartation by association.

The plane lifts off and I drive off wondering where all this will go.

The following week my secretary calls me, "Pastor, Greg Mauro is on the phone."

"Pastor Ford, Dr. Cerullo wanted me to call you to express his deepest gratitude for hosting the rally, he will be sending you a personal letter later this week. Pastor, Dr. Cerullo asked if you could **join him** in Nigeria and be one of the speakers with him for his 'Mission to all the World African Conference'." WOW – it's... Favor! Favor! Favor! Wow! It's, Yes!, Yes!, Yes!

What an awesome week it was, 39 thousand delegates from 22 African nations forever changed by God's anointing.

As if ministering with Brother Cerullo all week was not enough for God to do for me, He was about to do more. El-Shaddai (the God of more than enough) was about to bless me again beyond my imagination. (Ephesians 3:20)

Saturday morning, the closing session. "We will anoint each person personally with oil." WOW! Here we go again! How will seven people anoint 39 thousand? Simple, one at a time.

Get ready – Get set – Go! 7:00 a.m. until 1:00 p.m. we stand and anoint people. There were times my body would shake as if I could not go on. I would stop – wait upon the Holy

Spirit, then a surge of supernatural power would release and away we would go. All the while I am recalling Habakkuk 1:5 (Amp.) *"Look around you, ... replied the Lord, among the nations and see! And be astonished! Astounded! For I am putting into effect a work in your days such that you would not believe it if it were told you."*

39 thousand Africans from 22 nations forever transformed by the anointing.

As for me, I stand in awe at the mighty hand of God, as time after time He opens great and mighty doors for me to walk through.

What's next? Only God knows!

Allow me to leave you with the statement spoken to me by Morris Cerullo.

"Pastor Ford – **Power does not travel in words, but true power is manifest through relationship**." Each relationship positioning you to be...

FIRST ON THE SCENE

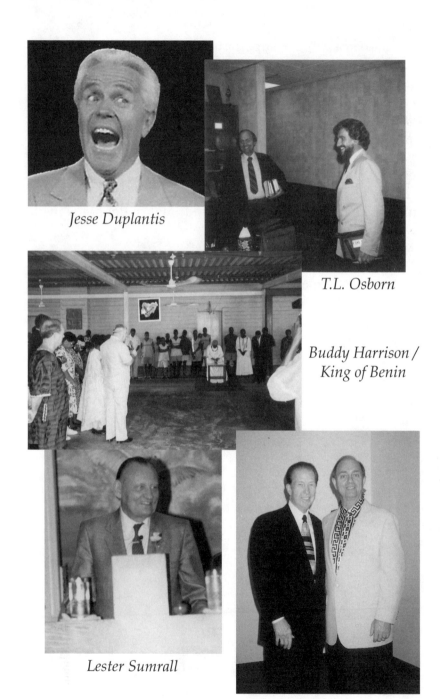

Jesse Duplantis

T.L. Osborn

Buddy Harrison /
King of Benin

Lester Sumrall

John Osteen

*Jerry and
Carolyn Savelle*

Tommy and Rachel Burchfield

Morris Cerullo

Jesse and Cathy Duplantis

T.L. and Daisy Osborn

Felix and Abiola Omobude and Buddy Harrison (center)

Bishop Mike and Peace Okonkwo

Conclusion

I feel like the apostle John when closing his writings, he said, "...*There are also many other things which Jesus did, that which, if they should be written every one, I suppose that even the world itself could not contain the book that should be written.*"

As I began this project, I realized that God had done so many things in and through my life. My life itself is like a great book, filled with struggles and filled with victories. Each struggle overcome by God's power. As I would think back and remember each encounter, it would only trigger a remembrance of another encounter too numerous to record.

We have a mission from God, as His children. Our mission is to reach out and touch. Touching people is our business. Changing people is our mission. The joy of seeing people whose lives are broken and torn, who have given up hope, suddenly touched by the hand of God, rising above the beggarly elements of life.

OUR MISSION?

M - is for making new roads. First, we must see the possibility for good in our world and make things happen for the betterment of humanity. Moving mountains.

I - is for inventing new solutions. We must see the needs of society and discover new ways to meet those needs. Insisting that the Word works in our lives.

S - is for saving new souls. It is seeing the waste of human lives without God and offering them the loving life force of Jesus Christ. Saving souls. Setting the captives free. Seeing the power of God come alive.

S - is for seeking new ideas. We see the unlimited potential of every person and sow new ideas of success in their mind, to become the best for God. Standing against satan and all of his evil forces.

I - is for inspiring new discoveries. It is seeing the loneliness of people, without purpose, and inspiring new discoveries of who they are in God. Involved with the Holy Ghost.

O - is for opening new doors. We see the lack of productivity of those who are locked into a poor image of themselves. We must open a new door of fulfillment through the loving service to other people. Obedience is the key to victory.

N - is for nourishng new dreams. It is seeing the destructiveness of negativism and nourishing dreams of positive living by faith in God. Now is the hour!

Our mission is to lift people to a love relationship with God.

I have seen millions of faces around the world reaching out to be touched by someone; the orphan child on the street, the lonely teenager looking for some meaning in life, another begging for bread, the wrinkled brow of a man wondering if he will be able to provide for his family that day. We have wept over the lame, the hurt, the blind, the deaf, and the dumb, as they have reached out to us with their eyes as if to say, "Are you the one? Are you the one that will touch us?" I have climbed the mountains of Guatemala to share Jesus with a people unknown to the outer world. I have walked in the lonely pueblos of Mexico. I have met an old woman named Sister Lupe, who would rise up early in the morning and travel into the hills by bus until it would travel no more. She would then walk back into the mountain villages, as all those who saw her would say, "Why do you travel so far?" Her reply, "I must go tell the children about Jesus, or He will forever be lost to the people."

I have walked the dirty Nile delta of Egypt and have seen the blind and sick children begging for bread. I have traveled the deep rivers of Venezuela by canoe for hours, to be met by a frail little lady and her five children standing by the banks of the river. I have heard her cry as she greeted us, "I've been waiting for you. God has answered my prayer." I broke when she handed me a coconut shell full of spaghetti to eat, knowing she had no more. I have traveled by night for hours to reach the dusty, dirty, dark villages of Africa, to be greeted by the rhythmic beat of the African drum as the people rejoice that someone has come. I have heard the wonderful cry, "You are welcome! You are welcome!"

I have seen the young teenager as he walked on all fours like a dog, because his body was broken at birth. I have seen the hundreds of children grab our hands and cry, "White man, white man!" Their cry to touch and be touched. I have seen the faces of the Pastor and his wife as tears would fill their eyes and hear them say, "If you must leave, will you come again?" I have wept over the nations and their people. I have sat silent for hours, as I traveled the roads of the world and the people stare at me with great wonder. I hear their cries day and night, "Are you the one? Are you the one that will touch us?"

That is why I have determined to be...

FIRST ON THE SCENE!

Your Personal Journey

There are no accidents with God! *"To every thing there is a season, and a time to every purpose under the heavens."* Ecclesiastes 3:1

This book reached your hands by divine guidance. Why? You have a divine appointment with destiny. (Jeremiah 29:11)

By now you surely realize that you have been "First on the Scene" many times in your life.

My prayer is that your faith has been ignited to new heights. That you are more determined now than ever before to reach out and change someone's life. Someone waits on the other side of your obedience.

You are a carrier of God's anointing. You are an infectious person, a pestilent fellow and a terror to hell.

The following pages are reserved for you to record **Your Personal Journey**. Those times that God will position you to be "First on the Scene." Your adventures in faith.

Now – Go take on the world!

My Adventures in Faith

I was
FIRST ON THE SCENE!

Notes: _____

_____

_____

_____

_____

_____

_____

_____

_____

_____

_____

_____

_____

_____

_____

_____

My Adventures in Faith

I was
FIRST ON THE SCENE!

Notes: _____

_____

_____

_____

_____

_____

_____

_____

_____

_____

_____

_____

_____

_____

_____

_____

My Adventures in Faith

I was
FIRST ON THE SCENE!

Notes: _____

_____

_____

_____

_____

_____

_____

_____

_____

_____

_____

_____

_____

_____

_____

_____

My Adventures in Faith

I was
FIRST ON THE SCENE!

Notes: _____

_____

_____

_____

_____

_____

_____

_____

_____

_____

_____

_____

_____

_____

_____

_____

_____

My Adventures in Faith

I was
FIRST ON THE SCENE!

Notes: _____

_____

_____

_____

_____

_____

_____

_____

_____

_____

_____

_____

_____

_____

_____

_____

_____

My Adventures in Faith

I was
FIRST ON THE SCENE!

Notes: _____

_____

_____

_____

_____

_____

_____

_____

_____

_____

_____

_____

_____

_____

_____

Richard Ford

Richard Ford is a God-called and seasoned Pastor, who along with his wife, Tena, have pastored Family Worship Center in Stafford, Texas since 1980. His heart stirring messages are changing the lives of many each day. Those that know him have said; he has the obedience of Abraham, the spirit of Joseph, the faithfulness of Paul, the submission of Timothy, the power of the Holy Ghost, and the compassion of Jesus, as he reaches out to the world.

He preaches the Word of God with a "Holy Ghost Fire" that transforms its hearers forever. He's Hell's greatest nightmare, yet, the father-like compassion of Christ is imparted from him to men, women, and children during their most desperate time of need.

Pastor Ford's heart's desire is to train and to equip members of the Body of Christ to become all that God purposes for them to be. His heart to win the lost is evident in his sermons and also in his calling to the foreign soils of the world where he has preached to the multitudes.

FAMILY WORSHIP CENTER

Our Reason For Being

To bring people to Jesus and membership in His family, develop them to Christ-like maturity, and equip them for their ministry in the church and life mission in the world, in order to magnify God's name.

The Vision

- To train His Army . . .
- To perfect the saints . . .
- To be ready for the harvest . . .
- To be a light to our city . . .
- To take the gospel to the world . . .
- To touch a hurting, sighing, dying, lost generation.

A Good Place to Call Home!